Pope Benedict XVI and the

SEXUAL ABUSE
CRISIS

Pope Benedict XVI and the Sexual Abuse Crisis

Working for Redemption and Renewal

Gregory Erlandson
and Matthew Bunson

Our Sunday Visitor Publishing Division
Our Sunday Visitor, Inc.
Huntington, Indiana 46750

Copyright © 2010 Our Sunday Visitor, Inc. Published 2010.

14 13 12 11 10   1 2 3 4 5 6 7

ISBN: 978-1-59276-806-6 (Inventory No. T1109)
LCCN: 2010926416

Cover design by Rebecca J. Heaston
Cover photo: Stefano Spaziani
Interior design by Sherri L. Hoffman

PRINTED IN THE UNITED STATES OF AMERICA

Contents

Foreword   9

Introduction   11

PART ONE — A Growing Awareness

Chapter One: The Rise of Joseph Ratzinger   17

Chapter Two: The Cardinal's "Conversion"   24

PART TWO — A Global Crisis

Chapter Three: A "Festering Disease"   41

Chapter Four: The Modern Sex Abuse Crisis   49

Chapter Five: A Worldwide Scandal   63

PART THREE — Benedict and the Road to Renewal

Chapter Six: "Where Do We Go from Here?"   77

Chapter Seven: The Way Forward   89

Chapter Eight: "I Share in Their Suffering"   98

Conclusion   117

Prayer for Pope Benedict XVI   128

APPENDICES

Appendix One: The Perspective of Canon Law   131
A Commentary on the motu proprio Sacramentorum
Sanctitatis Tutela *by Msgr. William King, J.C.D.*

Appendix Two: Guide to Understanding Basic CDF
Procedures concerning Sexual Abuse Allegations
(Released by the Vatican April 10, 2010)   146

STATEMENTS AND COMMENTARY

Commentary and Excerpts

Good Friday, 2005: Cardinal Joseph Ratzinger's Good
    Friday Meditations at the Stations of the Cross   151

October 28, 2006: Pope Benedict's XVI's *ad limina*
    address to the Irish bishops   158

April 15, 2008: Pope Benedict XVI's in-flight
    conference on his way to the United States   164

April 16, 2008: Pope Benedict XVI's address to the
    bishops of the United States at the Basilica of the
    National Shrine of the Immaculate Conception   169

April 17, 2008: Pope Benedict XVI's homily at the
    Mass at the Washington Nationals Stadium   177

April 19, 2008: Pope Benedict XVI's homily at
    St. Patrick's Cathedral   182

July 19, 2008: Pope Benedict XVI's homily at the
    Mass at the Cathedral of Sydney   187

Commentary and Full Text

March 19, 2010: Pope Benedict XVI's Pastoral Letter
    to the Catholics of Ireland   191

We dedicate this book to the tens of thousands of good priests who live their vows, love their people, and serve the Lord faithfully and well.

Lord, your Church often seems like a boat about to sink, a boat taking in water on every side. In your field we see more weeds than wheat.

— Joseph Cardinal Ratzinger,
Good Friday Meditation, 2005

I am ashamed and we will do everything possible to ensure that this does not happen in [the] future.

— Pope Benedict XVI, in-flight press conference
on his way to the United States, April 15, 2008

Foreword

This book arose out of a desire to help Catholics who have been shocked, disappointed, angered, or simply depressed by the latest round of allegations of clergy sexual abuse that have been filling our newspapers and our news channels. That such charges are now reaching up to the papacy itself has been incredibly dispiriting and disturbing. Scripture warns, "I will strike the shepherd, and the sheep of the flock will be dispersed" (Mt 26:31). Deluged by a 24/7 news cycle of leaks and allegations that is hard enough to keep up with, much less analyze or debate, many Catholics see the chief shepherd, the pope himself, as wounded, and his leadership has been questioned.

One of the lessons of the scandal is that the truth is not our enemy and is not to be feared. The facts must be faced, but they must also be examined with balance and honesty. Some are difficult to comprehend, and readers will find stories and accounts in the pages to follow that are as sickening as they are disheartening.

But the commitment to the truth also means getting the facts right and setting the record straight when needed. Many people have made terrible mistakes in the past, but much has been accomplished as well. We know from our own experience that sin is real, but so is repentance. With God's grace, the renewal of the Church is at hand, and Pope Benedict has played a pivotal role in leading the Church forward. This book will help you to understand what has taken place and where we are heading.

There will be more allegations, and the incidents in this book will be augmented by other investigations, further reforms, and continued self-reflection on the part of the Church. The Church, under the leadership of Pope Benedict XVI, has not and will not shy away from addressing the scandals and redressing the mistakes.

In the end, however, this book is also about hope and trust. As Catholics, we place both in the loving hands of the Holy Spirit. For two millennia, hope and trust have always been justified, despite the sins of popes, bishops, priests, and laypeople. The way forward will be difficult and painful. But the commitment to the truth will guide our path, and our trust and hope in the Holy Spirit will shield us in the dark days and lead us to a renewal of the entire People of God.

Gregory Erlandson
Matthew Bunson

Introduction

How do you respond when you learn that a brother, a sister, a son, or a daughter has been sexually abused?

What angry, even murderous thoughts, self-condemnation, and sense of failure for not having asked, not having known? What self-torture if your half-conscious instincts or nagging concerns had not been followed? What immense frustration that the person whom you wanted to protect more than anything was harmed on your watch, and nothing that you or a judge or a policeman can do will erase that despicable act or restore your loved one to wholeness.

The pain and betrayal of the victims is unimaginable. It is something that they will have to live with, a burden they will have to carry forever. But for the rest of us, it is all too easy to imagine how we would feel if our child was a victim.

The story of the sexual abuse crisis in the Church has been for so many Catholics one of betrayal, of failure, of insensitivity to profound suffering, and of wanton cruelty to the most defenseless among us, our children. We have read about the abuser priests, the failed efforts to treat them, the movement from parish to parish by bishops who seemed not to understand the damage that was done.

Most recently, there has been an enormous amount of discussion about whether Pope Benedict XVI was part of the problem.

The question was first asked in the wake of a story about the treatment of an abuser priest during the future pope's tenure as archbishop of Munich. That was followed by a *New York Times* story alleging, "Vatican Declined to Defrock U.S. Priest

Who Abused Boys." The story launched a torrent of claims by other news agencies and papers, and was soon amplified by television news media and endless blogs and Web sites.

The heavily repeated theme was twofold: That no progress has been made with regard to the Church's handling of the sex abuse crisis — that, if anything, it is getting worse. And second, that Joseph Ratzinger, as an archbishop in Germany, as a cardinal and head of the Vatican's Congregation for the Doctrine of the Faith, and now as pope, has committed acts of neglect, cover-up, and disregard for the plight of the victims of sexual abuse by the clergy.

Both assertions are false, but most readers, including most Catholics, might find it hard to find a contrary point of view and therefore have had little reason to doubt them as fact.

The result has been the defamation of one of the Church officials over the last decade who has understood clearly the scale of the crisis of sexual abuse and who has labored to end it and to reform the Church in such a way that it can never happen again — Pope Benedict XVI.

Likewise, the genuine record of progress has been completely neglected. For the last eight years, the Catholic Church in the United States has undergone a transformation through the application of the so-called Dallas Charter and the imposition of the Essential Norms, by which dioceses created safe environments for children, launched a "zero tolerance" policy regarding abuse, and worked to improve the formation of priests and seminary system. The results have been nothing short of dramatic.

However, with the latest accusations, it seems as though the last eight years and the progress made in them simply never happened.

Benedict XVI and the Sexual Abuse Crisis has been written to help return the focus to the genuine role Pope Benedict has played and continues to play in combating the scourge of sexual abuse in the Church, the way that he is working for reform and renewal, and the progress that has been achieved in curbing this blight on the priesthood and the Church. The main themes of this book are simple:

1. The Church has always been confronted by the problem of sexual sin and failings among its clergy, and while the number of abusers has never been large, the Church has labored over the centuries to curb such abuses.

2. Although modern Church leaders have made grievous mistakes, and the criminal acts of certain clergy have been overlooked or unaddressed in the past in too many dioceses, the Church is dedicated to redressing these wrongs and making sure that every safeguard is in place to protect children and families.

3. Cardinal Ratzinger became increasingly convinced of the need to rid the Church of what he called the "filth" of abuse, and emerged as one of the Vatican's most dedicated leaders in confronting the growing crisis.

4. Pope Benedict's actions in the first years of his pontificate showed a forthright desire to address the sexual abuse crisis in word and deed. He has continued to address the topic repeatedly and directly, in a variety of situations.

5. The United States Church, which was for several years at the epicenter of the scandals, is now leading the way in establishing norms and providing guidelines for dealing with priest abusers, assisting the victims, and preventing further crimes.

6. As Church leaders around the world confront the sexual abuse crisis in their own countries, they are looking to Pope Benedict for leadership and to the U.S. Church for a roadmap to reconciliation, reform, and authentic justice.

7. Pope Benedict is not only dedicated to ending abuse among the clergy but also sees that the Church must seek spiritual renewal if it is to be purified.

These themes are based on our study of the relevant Vatican documents and speeches of Pope Benedict, and we have included those texts near the end of this book for your study and review as well. In the appendix you will also find a commentary by a canon lawyer on Church law as it relates to the crisis. For additional information and updates, readers can go to www.popebenedictandabusecrisis.com.

Reform and renewal have gone hand in hand across the 2,000 years of Catholic history. While it is true that not all renewal comes from the top of the Church, authentic reform of and by the papacy has been crucial in providing impetus for such reform of the whole. Pope Benedict XVI, an expert in the writings of Augustine and the great Franciscan theologian Bonaventure, understands very well the power of reforming movements and the immense good that can come from renewal. As the pope wrote to Irish Catholics recently:

> I wish to exhort *all of you* . . . to reflect on the wounds inflicted on Christ's body, the sometimes painful remedies needed to bind and heal them, and the need for unity, charity and mutual support in the long-term process of restoration and ecclesial renewal.

This book does not claim to be an exhaustive study of the history of sexual sins in the Church or even of the sex abuse scandal that has bedeviled the Church for the last decades. That is another book to be written in the years to come. But it is our hope that after reading this book, you will have a renewed appreciation of the work of the pope — and the leaders of reform in the Church — and what they have managed to achieve in the last years.

PART ONE

A Growing Awareness

CHAPTER ONE

The Rise of Joseph Ratzinger

A bishop whose only concern is not to have any problems and to gloss over as many conflicts as possible is an image I find repulsive.

— Cardinal Joseph Ratzinger,
in *Salt of the Earth*

On April 13, 2010, the German police in the Bavarian town of Marktl-am-Inn reported that a small home had been vandalized. Obscene comments referring to Pope Benedict XVI's supposed failings in handling the sex abuse crisis had been spray painted in blue across the door.

Joseph Ratzinger was born in that home on Holy Saturday, April 16, 1927.

Ratzinger has been witness to many of the most significant events of the past century: The rise of Nazism; the division, and eventual unification, of Europe; the Second Vatican Council — and the fracturing of the Church afterward; and the pontificate of Pope John Paul II (1978-2005). His own ecclesiastical career has included immense achievements: serving as one of the leading theologians of the twentieth century, being appointed as archbishop of Munich and Freising in his native Germany, becoming a member of the College of Cardinals and prefect of the Congregation for the Doctrine of the Faith — and, finally, being elected pope on April 19, 2005.

But — as with so many leaders of the Church in the past twenty-five years — the many accomplishments of this theologian, cardinal, Vatican official, and pope may be tarnished by the clergy sexual abuse scandal, just as the house of his birth was smeared by the vandal's paintbrush. In the case of Joseph Ratzinger, now Pope Benedict XVI, this will be a painful irony, for it has been under his leadership that the Vatican realized the scope of the problem facing the Church and began to take steps to address its impact.

Joseph Ratzinger was born into a devout Catholic family in a small town in Bavaria, Germany's most Catholic region. His father was a police official, his mother a hotel cook. Joseph was only five years old when the turmoil facing Germany began to impact his family. In 1932, his father foresaw the rising political and cultural power of the National Socialist Party, the Nazis, and sought to move away from its influence by relocating to a town called Aschau-am-Inn.

For young Joseph, it was here that he came to appreciate his Catholic faith, attending Mass with his family and praying the rosary daily. When he was twelve years old, he decided to enter the seminary, following in the footsteps of his brother, Georg.

Like his brother, Joseph was forced to enroll in the Hitler Youth as a high school seminarian. In a 1997 book-length interview with journalist Peter Seewald, *Salt of the Earth*, Cardinal Ratzinger recalled his distaste at this requirement, and he limited his participation to the minimal amount required.

In 1943, when Joseph was sixteen, the seminarians were conscripted into an anti-aircraft brigade in Munich. He was transferred the next year to a military work brigade on the Austria-Hungary border. He recalls that, as the tide of war turned, an anti-Nazi officer sent him home. When Germany fell, he was put into an American prisoner of war camp for a short while and then released on June 19, 1945.

Ratzinger was never a member of the Nazi party, and the war had ended by the time he was eighteen. So, the emphasis on his alleged "Nazi past" — repeatedly mentioned by critics

as a way to cast aspersions on his character and .
outlook — is at its heart a charge without merit.
With the war over, Joseph and his brothei
the seminary, where Joseph was soon recognized ı
ligence and joined a theological institute associate   ᴧ the
University of Munich. The Ratzinger brothers were ordained
together on June 29, 1951.

In graduate studies at the University of Munich, Joseph
Ratzinger focused on St. Augustine, one of the great doctors of
the Church. In a 2004 talk, Cardinal Ratzinger explained part
of what fascinated him about the fourth-century theologian:

> Augustine, who lived in an age very similar to our own,
> went so far as to describe wisdom as a "foreign word."

Perhaps recalling his own experiences of Marxism and Nazism,
Ratzinger said of the saint:

> Experiencing the great emptiness of the ideologies of
> his time, Augustine felt a great thirst for that Truth that
> opens the way to Life. He understood that no one is able
> to reach God by his own efforts, and he discovered in the
> end that Christ is the true Wisdom.

The young Ratzinger was recognized as a brilliant theologian, his star rising in a field of theological luminaries that
included Hans Küng and Karl Rahner. Many of these theologians were about to experience the highlight of their careers,
the Second Vatican Council, which began in 1962.

For Ratzinger, as for many others, this was an opportunity
for genuine reform and renewal in the Church. Ratzinger was
part of a generation of theologians seeking to engage the modern world. Pope John XXIII had expressed the wider movement under the title of *aggiornamento* (bringing up to date),
which was his desire to have the Council proclaim the timeless
truths of the Church in ways comprehensible to the modern

world. The parameters of traditional scholastic theology — oriented toward intellectual formulas and analogies — seemed inadequate; many, among them Ratzinger, sought to recover the wisdom of the Church Fathers — the earliest leaders and theologians of the Church, such as St. Augustine. Ratzinger described this return to the Fathers, an enterprise often termed *resourcement*, in an interview with Peter Seewald:

> I was of the opinion that scholastic theology, in the form it had come to have, was no longer an instrument for bringing faith into the contemporary discussion. It had to get out of its armor; it also had to face the situation of the present in a new language, in a new openness. So a greater freedom also had to arise in the Church.

Ratzinger was appointed a *peritus,* or expert advisor, to the German bishops attending the council — who in turn played an influential role in the creation of key conciliar documents. Karol Wojtyla, the future Pope John Paul II, was a bishop at the same council, although there was no record of the two future popes meeting each other there.

That Ratzinger was a voice for reform during the Council, there is no doubt. But he did not see the Council as a break with the teachings or Tradition of the Church. Rather, he saw it as a recovery of profound truths, "to update the faith . . . in order to present it with its full impact."

For Ratzinger, his strongly held belief — shaped by the radical politics that soon engulfed Western Europe, particularly the universities — was that the Council, properly understood, would preserve one from extremism of any sort. He also believed that the Council Fathers neither intended any rupture with the past nor were somehow dismissive of the twenty other ecumenical councils that had gone before it.

Unfortunately, he came to see relatively quickly that the Council was being understood less as a deepening or even a "radicalization of the faith," than as a kind of "dilution of the faith" in the form of concessions and adaptations to the modern world. As with many of the theologians of his generation, one could argue that the rest of his theological career has been engaged in the battle over how to understand the documents of the Second Vatican Council.

After the Council, Ratzinger encountered the extremism firsthand with clashes with radical students at the University of Tübingen, where Marxism held great sway among theologians as well. This experience was closely followed by the worldwide dissent that followed the release of Pope Paul VI's controversial encyclical, *Humanae Vitae* (1968), reaffirming and elaborating on the Church's defense of the unitive and procreative aspects of marital love and opposition to artificial birth control.

In the 1970s, Ratzinger became engaged in a project of rearticulating the Christian faith for modern men and women. Perhaps his most important book in this regard was *Introduction to Christianity*. Focusing on his teaching and his theology, he served as a member of the International Theological Commission, a Vatican advisory group that examines significant theological issues of the day.

Ratzinger's life as a theologian and teacher took an unexpected turn in 1977, however, when Pope Paul VI appointed him archbishop of the archdiocese of Munich and Freising, a diocese first established in the eighth century. At barely fifty years old, with no chancery and little pastoral experience, he would assume leadership of one of Germany's most historic archdioceses. At the time of his appointment, Munich had 2.2 million Catholics (75 percent of the population) and more than 1,700 priests.

Lest there be any doubt about Pope Paul's high esteem for the Bavarian theologian, Ratzinger was named a cardinal only a few days after his ordination as archbishop.

In 1978, the year of three popes, Cardinal Ratzinger participated in the two papal elections (called conclaves) that followed the death of Paul VI. At the first, Pope John Paul I was elected, but his death one month later led to the historic election of the first non-Italian in more than 400 years: Karol Wojtyla, Pope John Paul II.

Prior to 1978, Ratzinger and Wojtyla were aware of each other's work, but due to the Communist grip on Eastern Europe, they had not met in person. Their first meeting took place at the first conclave in 1978. It has been reported that Cardinal Ratzinger was a supporter of Wojtyla in the second conclave and was pleased at his election.

Pope John Paul II was quick to see him as an ally, and Cardinal Ratzinger became head of the International Theological Commission for the new pontiff. He was invited to travel with the pope, both to Germany and on his historic first visit to Communist Poland. When the pope offered him the post of Prefect of the Congregation for Catholic Education in 1980, Ratzinger said he had not spent enough time in Munich, but in 1981 he accepted appointment as prefect (or head) of the Congregation for the Doctrine of the Faith.

Known in Vatican shorthand as the CDF, the Congregation has as its primary responsibility the safeguarding of Church teachings in the areas of faith and morals. Journalists often like to allude to its ominous title of centuries past — the Office of the Holy Inquisition. Despite the changes in the name, however, the Office's focus remains on theological opinions and writings, and on guiding, investigating, and — at times — admonishing those who seek to study and articulate the teachings of the Faith.

In the words of *Pastor Bonus*, the Apostolic Constitution on the Roman Curia, published in 1988:

> The duty proper to the Congregation for the Doctrine of the Faith is to promote and safeguard the doctrine of the faith and morals throughout the Catholic world: for

this reason everything which in any way touches upon such matters falls within its competence.

It is under this mandate that the Congregation would become increasingly involved in the clergy sexual abuse cases that were to rock the Church in the 1990s.

CHAPTER TWO

The Cardinal's "Conversion"

It is understandable that you find it hard to forgive or be reconciled with the Church. In her name, I openly express the shame and remorse that we all feel. At the same time, I ask you not to lose hope.

— Pope Benedict XVI, Pastoral Letter to the
Catholics of Ireland, March 19, 2010

As head of the Congregation for the Doctrine of the Faith, Cardinal Ratzinger faced many challenges in the 1980s over doctrinal matters — the battle over Marxist-influenced liberation theology, the revolution in bioethical issues such as *in vitro* fertilization, and concerns about the teachings of other theologians, often described as "progressive," who were accused of dissenting from Church teaching. The Congregation also addressed a wide range of issues involving Catholic practice, including the reception of the Eucharist by the divorced and remarried.

In 1986, the Congregation's statement on homosexuality, labeling it an objective disorder, provoked a great deal of controversy. But the Congregation also addressed related themes regarding discrimination against homosexuals and homosexuals in the seminary.

In his interview with Raymond Arroyo on EWTN in 2003, then-Cardinal Ratzinger summed up the responsibilities of the CDF:

We have essentially and often to do with all the problems of the Church — problems of relativism, of heresies, of unacceptable theologies, difficult theologians and so on. Also with the disciplinary cases, also problem of pedophiles is our problem. We are really in this Congregation confronted with the most difficult aspects of the life of the Church today.

With its two responsibilities being doctrinal and disciplinary matters, the Congregation is guaranteed to be involved in almost all of the major controversies facing the Church, and so it has been. With regard to clergy sexual abuse cases, however, the road did not immediately lead to the Congregation. While that had been the procedure in decades past, most cases involving the disciplining and possible dismissal from the clerical state (often termed "laicization" or "defrocking" by the secular media) for sins of sexual abuse were directed to the Congregation for the Clergy, and some to the Tribunal of the Roman Rota. The Congregation for the Clergy is the administrative organ of the Roman Curia that deals principally with issues surrounding churches and parish life, including many topics of priestly life. Only if the abuse involved solicitations in the confessional or the improper use of absolution for a sexual partner did the Congregation for the Doctrine of the Faith get involved in the case.

Initially, as the United States dioceses found themselves in the throes of lawsuits regarding clergy sexual abuse scandals, Vatican officials seemed too often to be dismissive of the wider implications of the cases. Ratzinger himself reportedly told a group of Spanish Catholics that the U.S. media was exaggerating the story for its own ends. Perhaps most controversial was the comment by Cardinal Dario Castrillon de Hoyos in 2002, blaming the clergy sexual abuse scandals on a culture of "pan sexuality and sexual licentiousness."

As Cardinal Ratzinger and his staff became aware of the breadth and depth of the abuse problem, however, it was clear that its impact on him led him to cease making efforts to blame the crisis on the media messenger. He had undergone what John Allen, a longtime commentator on Vatican matters, called Ratzinger's "conversion experience." At the heart of that "conversion" was the CDF's increasing immersion in the clergy abuse cases after Pope John Paul assigned it responsibility to oversee all of the cases worldwide.

On May 18, 2001, the pope promulgated an apostolic letter called *Sacramentorum Sanctitatis Tutela* ("The Safeguarding of the Sacraments"). The document, which had been in drafting and broad consultation for several years, was most noteworthy for the fact that it confirmed the CDF's responsibility for disciplinary review and action regarding violations associated with abuse, including the solicitation to a sexual sin (a sin "against the Sixth Commandment") under the pretext of the confession if involving the confessor himself or the granting of absolution to "an accomplice" in a sexual sin by the confessor.

It also said that it reserved to the CDF the responsibility for reviewing sexual violations "committed by a cleric with a minor below the age of eighteen years." Such acts are "to be punished according to the gravity of the offense, not excluding dismissal or deposition." In canon law, the age of a minor was listed as below sixteen years. In the 1990s the U.S. bishops had asked that the age of a minor be defined as under eighteen, so that it would match state law in defining the upper age of minors. The apostolic letter also addressed a long-standing request by U.S. bishops that the statute of limitations be lengthened — in this case for ten years, rather than five — after the victim has reached his or her eighteenth birthday.

In short, what the apostolic letter did was require bishops to report cases of clergy sexual abuse to the CDF.

In a letter to the world's bishops at the time of the document's release, Cardinal Ratzinger explained that while probable cases had to be reported to the CDF, the Congregation could allow the cases to be held in the local diocese or bring the case before its own tribunal. While canon law, particularly canon 1395, has made clear that the sexual abuse of minors by clerics is a violation of law, the new procedures created a more effective process for the large number of cases being uncovered. By requiring that such cases be reported to Rome, it also addressed concerns that abuse cases were being handled differently in different dioceses and countries.

The apostolic letter was not without its critics. Some initially wanted the statute of limitations to be longer, while the requirement that the cases be "subject to pontifical secret" raised concerns about transparency. Defenders of the letter stressed that the requirement was really one of confidentiality for both the accuser and the accused — it did not in any way preclude notifying civil authorities — but such language was understandably confusing to some.

In an interview with Vatican Radio on January 10, 2002, as reported by Catholic News Service, Archbishop (now Cardinal) Tarcisio Bertone, then-secretary of the doctrinal congregation, said the new norms reflected Vatican concern about the scandal caused by sex abuse cases against minors:

> There have emerged some cases of gravely illicit behavior on the part of ordained ministers. We know these cases are given emphasis and highlighted by the media and the press, and, therefore, in a sense provoke more scandal than in the past, when information about this kind of behavior was considered confidential.
>
> Therefore, the problem of scandal is a problem that worries the church.

Archbishop Bertone said it was especially unfortunate that the priestly ministry as a whole had been "offended" by the behavior of "a few persons, a few ministers, when almost the totality of ministers behaves in an exemplary manner."

According to a 2005 *New York Times* report, Cardinal Ratzinger reviewed the allegations of clergy abuse every Friday morning. "He found the cases so disturbing he called the work 'our Friday penance.'"

In his March 17, 2010, column for the *National Catholic Reporter*, John Allen said Cardinal Ratzinger soon came to know more about the scale and scope of the scandals than anyone else in the Church:

> By all accounts, Ratzinger was punctilious about studying the files, making him one of the few churchmen anywhere in the world to have read the documentation on virtually every Catholic priest ever credibly accused of sexual abuse. As a result, he acquired a familiarity with the contours of the problem that virtually no other figure in the Catholic Church can claim.

Allen said that Cardinal Ratzinger and his staff "seemed driven by a convert's zeal to clean up the mess":

> Of the 500-plus cases that the Congregation for the Doctrine of the Faith dealt with prior to Benedict's election to the papacy, the substantial majority were returned to the local bishop authorizing immediate action against the accused priest — no canonical trial, no lengthy process, just swift removal from ministry and, often, expulsion from the priesthood. In a more limited number of cases, the congregation asked for a canonical trial, and in a few cases the congregation ordered the priest reinstated.

> That marked a stark reversal from the initial insistence of Vatican officials, Ratzinger included, that in almost

every instance the accused priest deserved the right to canonical trial. Having sifted through the evidence, Ratzinger and [Msgr. Charles J.] Scicluna apparently drew the conclusion that in many instances the proof was so overwhelming that immediate action was required. Among insiders, the change of climate was dramatic.

In 2004, after Cardinal Ratzinger had had extensive experience reviewing the hundreds of case files of priests charged with sexual abuse, he agreed to meet with the National Review Board established by the U.S. bishops in 2002 to oversee their efforts to investigate the crisis.

The Board, which was then headed by Judge Anne Burke of Chicago, met with Cardinal Ratzinger for more than two hours. According to Judge Burke, the cardinal was informed, attentive, and supportive:

> Cardinal Ratzinger was far more open to meeting with members of the national review board than our own bishops and cardinals. He took in everything we had to say and answered our questions. And we pulled no punches: We told him what was going on in terms of the extent of the actual abuse by the priests and about our dismay with the U.S. Church hierarchy.

His cognizance of the profound nature of clergy sexual abuse was expressed most famously on Good Friday 2005, when Ratzinger conducted the Way of the Cross at the Colosseum in Rome for the frail Pope John Paul II. The cardinal wrote meditations for each of the Stations of the Cross, and for the Ninth Station, used words widely understood to refer to the abuse scandal: "How much filth there is in the Church, and even among those who, in the priesthood, ought to belong entirely to him!"

In February 2010, a Vatican official with the CDF spoke with Italian journalist Gianni Cardinale about the work of the CDF with abuse cases. The interview, published in the daily Catholic newspaper *L'Avvenire*, was unusual in the amount of detail that Msgr. Charles J. Scicluna — a promoter of justice, or a type of prosecutor for the tribunal of the CDF for these grave cases — gave.

According to Msgr. Scicluna, the Congregation has dealt with about 3,000 cases of diocesan and religious order priests who have been accused of sexual violations between 2001 and 2010; the crimes alleged have been committed over the past fifty years. (The priest described a "great wave of cases [that] flooded over our desks" in 2003 and 2004, most of them from the United States.) Of those 3,000 cases, 60 percent involved sexual attraction towards adolescents of the same sex; 30 percent involved heterosexual relations; and the remaining 10 percent were cases of pedophilia, or sexual attraction toward prepubescent children. There have been 300 cases of priests accused of pedophilia.

Of the 3,000 cases passed on to the Congregation, he went on to explain, 20 percent of them (about 600) have had full trials, with most of those in the "diocese of origin" but under the supervision of the CDF. He said that this helped to speed up the process.

From the point of view of the Church, the most severe censure is that of dismissal from the clerical state. The pope has done this in 10 percent of the cases — "the particularly serious ones in which the proof is overwhelming." In another 10 percent, such as in cases where priests have been arrested for the possession of child pornography, the priests themselves request laicization and it is granted. In addition, there are the civil charges that must be faced by those priests guilty of various crimes.

Sixty percent of cases have not been tried owing to the advanced age of the accused (most cases, of course, were for actions decades before), although various penalties have still been imposed, including the requirement that they may not celebrate Mass publicly or hear confessions, and must live in seclusion and prayer. This does not suggest that they have escaped justice on the part of the Church or criminal laws of their own countries. As Scicluna explained:

> It must be made absolutely clear that in these cases, some of which are particularly sensational and have caught the attention of the media, no absolution has taken place. It's true that there has been no formal condemnation, but if a person is obliged to a life of silence and prayer, then there must be a reason.

Msgr. Scicluna also addressed the question of whether bishops must inform authorities of allegations made against their priests. In countries where this is mandated, such as France, he said, bishops must cooperate with authorities. But he acknowledged that the difficulty is that the relationship between bishop and priest, as the Church understands it, is not so much employer and employee as filial — father and son.

To turn in a priest, he said,

> . . . is an onerous duty because the bishops are forced to make a gesture comparable to that of a father denouncing his own son. Nonetheless, our guidance in these cases is to respect the law.

In those countries where there is no such legal requirement, the CDF invites bishops to remind the victims and their families of their possible rights to report crimes. In all cases, they are to provide spiritual assistance (and more) to those so horribly afflicted by abuse.

Finally, most of the cases overseen by the CDF have come from the United States, although this share has decreased steadily since the peak years of 2003-2004. The overall number of cases must also be understood within the context of 400,000 priests worldwide. And the magnitude of the task involved must also be understood: Msgr. Scicluna indicated that nine officials — eight priests, including himself, and a lay lawyer — are in charge of the conduct of the massive caseload and trials.

As journalist John Allen noted, what is striking about these statistics is the evidence that Rome is willing to forgo trials in order to speed the process. Despite fears to the contrary in 2001 and 2002, the Vatican has allowed bishops to take immediate disciplinary action in 60 percent of the cases.

Msgr. Scicluna's interview helps to provide context for one of the most explosive cases to be reported on in the past year.

On March 25, 2010, the *New York Times* headlined, "Vatican declined to defrock priest who molested boys," on a story that began:

> Top Vatican officials — including the future Pope Benedict XVI — did not defrock a priest who molested as many as 200 deaf boys, even though several American bishops repeatedly warned them that failure to act on the matter could embarrass the church, according to church files newly unearthed as part of a lawsuit.

The case involves a priest of the archdiocese of Milwaukee, a Fr. Lawrence Murphy, who, from the 1950s until the mid-1970s, was alleged to have molested as many as 200 deaf students. Although there were reportedly complaints about Fr. Murphy in the 1960s, it was a complaint in 1974 that led to the priest taking a sick leave and moving to the Superior diocese, where he lived in his family's home with his mother. Although he had no official duties with the archdiocese of Milwaukee, the *Times* reported that there are allegations that he continued to abuse children in his new location.

In 1980, the Superior diocese contacted Milwaukee to ask what ministry the priest might undertake, and Archbishop Weakland, who had headed the archdiocese since 1977, responded that he should not be allowed to work with deaf children.

The story mentions only in passing that the police and prosecutors ignored the complaints of the victims for several decades; it also does not address why the archdiocese of Milwaukee, which had known about the case since the mid-1970s, did not choose to initiate any sort of proceedings against the priest until 1996. It was at that time that Archbishop Weakland wrote to the Congregation for the Doctrine of the Faith that he had just learned that some of the alleged abuses were to have taken place in the confessional — but this had been part of the original charges made in 1974.

Although the Congregation for the Doctrine of the Faith did not have responsibility at this point for abuse cases, because of the violation of the confessional, it did have authority to investigate the issue. The local bishop also had the right to initiate a Church trial on his own (this did not change until the 2001 apostolic letter), and Milwaukee notified Fr. Murphy that it was initiating such a trial. Then-Archbishop Bertone, who was the secretary for the Congregation at this time (and is now the Vatican's Secretary of State), wrote to Archbishop Weakland in 1997, approving of the trial.

Such a trial involves interviews with witnesses and the taking of testimony. These interviews were conducted between 1996 and 1998 by Fr. Thomas Brundage, the presiding judge in the case. He said the interviews "were the darkest days of my own priesthood," and called them "gut wrenching."

Then, in January 1998, Fr. Murphy wrote to Cardinal Ratzinger. He told the cardinal he was in ill health, that he had repented, and asked that he live out his final days in peace. Archbishop Bertone wrote to Archbishop Weakland to suggest that because of Fr. Murphy's declining health and the lack of charges filed in the previous twenty-five years, he be stripped of any ministerial duties. There was a discussion between the archdiocese of Milwaukee, the diocese of Superior, and Archbishop Bertone, resulting in Archbishop Weakland's decision in August 1998 to halt the trial and use other means to remove Fr. Murphy from ministry. Fr. Murphy died on Aug. 21, 1998, at the age of 72. What the *New York Times* did not report was that the auxiliary bishop of Milwaukee, Bishop Richard Sklba, celebrated the funeral Mass.

The Murphy case is one more example of the poor oversight and inadequate communication that typified many abuse cases in U.S. dioceses in the past fifty years. While a great deal of information was known about his actions from complaints received by students, actions to isolate the priest were ineffective, and there was little follow-up on the part of local Church authorities.

What the case does *not* show, however, is that Cardinal Ratzinger was somehow tolerant of, or insensitive to, the actions of abusers.

While there is no correspondence from Cardinal Ratzinger himself to Archbishop Weakland, the Congregation did support Archbishop Weakland's belated request for a Church trial, and then sought other, more immediate means to isolate the offending priest when it was clear that he was in poor health. According to the newspaper, it was Archbishop Weakland who was moved to take action out of concern for a lawsuit and his apparently belated discovery that the 1974 complaints had mentioned his abuse within the context of the confessional.

Dismissing a priest from the clerical state, as has been explained, is the most serious action that can be taken by the Church, and it is done only after a thorough inquest has been held. But the story shows that the Congregati work with Archbishop Weakland and had app trial. Only upon learning that the priest was dy gest a more rapid way to resolve the situation by 1 from ministry.

Like so many of the most heinous stories of clergy abuse — such as the cases in Boston and Fall River, but elsewhere as well — the story of Father Lawrence Murphy is revolting. But the *Times'* effort to pin responsibility for the case on Cardinal Ratzinger and the Congregation for the Doctrine of the Faith is clearly unfair.

As the current archbishop of Milwaukee, Jerome Listecki, put it:

> The mistakes [regarding the Murphy case] were not made in Rome in 1996, 1997, and 1998. The mistakes were made here, in the archdiocese of Milwaukee, in the 1970s, the 1980s, and the 1990s, by the church, by civil authorities, by church officials, and by bishops. And for that I beg your forgiveness.

Cardinal William Levada, who replaced Cardinal Ratzinger as head of the CDF, also published a highly unusual critique of the *Times'* allegations that was posted on the official Vatican Web site. Instead of blaming Cardinal Ratzinger for belated steps taken by the Milwaukee archdiocese in 1996 — twenty-two years after the archdiocese acknowledged becoming aware of the case — Cardinal Levada said that Pope Benedict should be acknowledged for what he has done to make the Church more responsive to abuse cases and their victims:

> We owe Pope Benedict a great debt of gratitude for introducing the procedures that have helped the Church to take action in the face of the scandal of priestly sexual abuse of minors. These efforts began when the Pope served as Cardinal Prefect of the Congregation for the

Doctrine of the Faith and continued after he was elected Pope.

In the weeks that followed, the Associated Press and other news organizations, under various headlines such as "Future Pope Stalled Pedophile Case," reported on the "smoking guns" of documents alleging the supposed willingness of Cardinal Ratzinger and Vatican officials to "stall" the cases dealing with priestly pedophilia. (Perhaps the worst example was MSNBC, which ran an article on its Web site titled "Pope Describes Touching Boys: I Went Too Far." The article it linked to had nothing to do with the pope, and the network later issued an apology when challenged by the Catholic League for Religious and Civil Rights.)

The Associated Press pointed to several cases, such as Fr. Michael Teta of Tucson, Arizona, and Fr. Stephen Kiesle of Oakland, California, in which years passed between the first reports of charges and the imposition of ecclesiastical penalties or dismissal from the clerical state. In the case of Kiesle, Cardinal Ratzinger's name appears on one letter out of thousands of documents, taken out of the context of the case, and without any effort to explain the legal system then in place when a priest requested to be laicized. John Norton, editor of *Our Sunday Visitor* newsweekly, points out that once again, the problem appeared to have been more on the American side than the Roman:

> The diocese of Oakland had every means at its disposal to contain the threat of Kiesle to children — but apparently did a very poor job of using them.
>
> It could have opened a Church trial to dismiss Kiesle from the clerical state. Apparently it did not. Granted, Kiesle could have appealed that sentence to a Church court in Rome, a process that is also very lengthy and with apparently unpredictable results [since this was before the 2001 changes]. . . . The diocese of Oakland could have

stripped Kiesle of his faculties and removed him from all ministry. But one of the documents shows the outrage of the diocesan director of youth ministry that Kiesle was still participating in parish youth ministry events, apparently even after the bishop and other diocesan officials had been notified.

The point is: Granting Kiesle's petition to be dispensed from the clerical state would have had no practical effect in containing the danger that he posed to youth. In fact, not doing so allowed the diocese to keeper tighter control over Kiesle's activities — and it looks like they fumbled.

A form letter, sent out to the parties involved at the start of the process of laicization, is now taken as evidence of Ratzinger's deliberate effort to protect a pedophile. Jeffrey Lena, the Vatican lawyer in the United States, argued in an interview with Reuters that the letter did not show "then-Cardinal Ratzinger resisting pleas from the bishop to defrock the priest. . . . There may be some overstep and rush to judgment going on here." The attorney added:

> During the entire course of the proceeding the priest remained under the control, authority and care of the local bishop who was responsible to make sure he did no harm, as the canon (Church) law provides. The abuse case wasn't transferred to the Vatican at all.

One issue rarely noted is that the "great wave of cases" (to use Msgr. Scicluna's phrase) threatened to overwhelm the CDF's small staff. In a recent column in *The Tablet*, Dominican Fr. Timothy Radcliffe, head of the Order of Preachers from 1992 to 2001, discussed the issue of the CDF's tiny staff and massive workload:

> It is generally imagined that the Vatican is a vast and efficient organization. In fact it is tiny. The CDF only

employs 45 people, dealing with doctrinal and disciplinary issues for a Church which has 1.3 billion members, 17 per cent of the world's population, and some 400,000 priests. When I dealt with the CDF as Master of the Dominican Order, it was obvious that they were struggling to cope. Documents slipped through the cracks. Cardinal Joseph Ratzinger lamented to me that the staff was simply too small for the job.

This was also a staff that had the duty of overseeing a host of demands and crises — from dissenting theologians to liberation theology, assisting the wider program of the Church envisioned by John Paul II, and answering questions from literally all over the world.

The other backdrop for these events is that as head of the CDF, Cardinal Ratzinger was aware of the need for constant renewal and reform for the Church. In words that are especially apt for today, he reflected upon the meaning of the maxim, "*Semper Ecclesia Reformanda*" (the Church is always needful of reform) in a 1985 interview with Italian journalist Vittorio Messori in *The Ratzinger Report*:

> The Church presumed that anyone who celebrated the Eucharist would need to say: *I* have sinned, Lord, look not upon *my* sins. It was the obligatory invocation of every priest; each bishop, the pope himself like the least priest, had to pronounce it in his daily Mass. And also the laity, all the other members of the Church, were called to unite themselves to that recognition of guilt. Therefore, *everybody* in the Church, with no exception, had to confess himself a sinner, beseech forgiveness and then set out on the path of real reform. But this in no way means that the Church as such was also a sinner. . . . In fact, in order to obtain Christ's forgiveness, my sin was set over against the *faith of his Church.*

PART TWO

A Global Crisis

CHAPTER THREE

A "Festering Disease"

How much filth there is in the Church, and even among
those who, in the priesthood, ought to belong entirely to
him!

— Joseph Cardinal Ratzinger,
Good Friday Meditation, 2005

The simple truth about the scandals facing the Church is that they're not new. From the earliest days of the Church, sins and failings among the ministers have been present in the life of the Christian faith. Church authorities clearly recognize this and have made many efforts over the centuries to assist those called to the priesthood and religious life in adhering to their vows and their commitment. These efforts include both spiritual support and, if necessary, penalties and disciplines for those who have failed to live up to their promises — especially for ministers who commit sins and crimes against the most defenseless, or abuse their power for personal gain or to satisfy their own predilections.

One of the ways that ministers have failed is in sexual abuse. While sexual abuse of minors is a significant social problem, and is better documented than ever before, the sexual abuse of minors by Catholic clergy has never been epidemic. A small percentage of priests and clergy over the centuries have violated the trust of the Church and those placed in its care, but the Church has never been tolerant of such actions. The

Church has insisted that priests live up to their vows and be free of the stain of abuse.

In dealing with the problem, limited as it has been, the Church has always tried to balance mercy for the sinner with justice for those who have suffered because of sexual sins. Success in rooting out and preventing clergy abuse has depended on vigilance, adherence to standing Church laws and norms, and sensible updating of oversight and priestly formation, as needed, to meet different circumstances and eras.

The renewal of the Church over the centuries has often included a reminder of those expectations by dedicated reformers.

In the New Testament, St. Paul exhorted those called to be ministers in the Christian community to live up to the demands of service in the Church. He stated in his first epistle to Timothy that bishops should be "without reproach" and deacons must be "serious, not double-tongued, not addicted to much wine, not greedy for gain . . . [and] must hold the mystery of faith with a clear conscience" (1 Tim 3:2, 8-9). That Paul felt it necessary to make such exhortations suggests he thought they were needed.

The Council of Elvira (held perhaps around 306 or 308 in Spain), although not a general (or ecumenical) council bringing together all the Church's bishops under the pope, is often cited as the first major Church gathering that imposed the requirement of priestly celibacy. Elvira was also notable for its extensive canons on discipline for the ministers of the Church and on sexual immorality. These were deemed necessary because of the huge number of conversions to the Church taking place among the pagan Romans and the need to reform a Roman culture deeply troubled by rampant sexual problems and lack of respect for the dignity of the human person: abortion, euthanasia, killing children by exposure, adultery, and homosexuality were generally accepted by all classes of Roman citizens.

It was especially important, then, that bishops, priests, and deacons live up to the demands of their ordination, and the canons included prohibitions against immorality, fornication, and adultery.

Not long after the Council at Elvira was the Council of Nicaea in 325, the first general council in the history of the Church. While summoned to deal with the heresy of Arianism, Nicaea also issued a series of canons on Church discipline and the proper preparation of those to be ordained. One of its canons forbade priests from living with any woman save for a close relative. Another called for adequate preparation for those to be ordained; another prohibited a priest from lending with interest, both to prevent usury and to prevent a priest from being able to hold a debt over a person, and thus have abusive power in a relationship.

The history of the succeeding councils and the development of Church law (or canon law) testifies to the fact that Church leaders were consistently concerned with the well-being of their priests and the protection of the faithful from the failures of some Church-appointed ministers who had fallen into frightful states of sin. Local councils or gatherings of bishops passed disciplinary decrees and canons that enforced or encouraged clerical celibacy and that imposed strong prohibitions against concubinage (or cohabitation with a woman), homosexuality, adultery, and fornication.

That the clerical abuse of children was deemed truly important to eradicate is made clear by one of the Church Fathers, St. Basil of Caesarea (d. 379). He wrote that any priest or monk found guilty of sexually molesting young boys should not only be removed from the clerical state but should also face physical punishments, such as public flogging and incarceration for six months — after which they were to undergo long and prayer-filled penances under the stern supervision of spiritual authorities. Above all, Basil urged, the priest or monk so convicted should never be permitted contact with, or have access to, young boys or men.

To assist confessors during the early Middle Ages in dealing with the needs of those seeking penance, manuals called *Penitentials* were developed in the Irish monasteries around the fifth century. One of the most famous was attributed to the great English monk, writer, and historian, Bede (d. c. 753). The *Penitentials* included among their suggested penances those for priests who were guilty of terrible sins, such as sodomy with children, especially young boys. The penalties were harsh, especially for bishops, and much more severe than for similar acts committed by laypeople.

Centuries later, as the leaders developed a clearer set of laws for the Church in the form of canon law, new prohibitions and condemnations were made of all forms of clergy sexual abuse. One of the most significant was during the time of Pope Leo IX, elected in 1049, at a time when the Church was in dire need of reform and renewal. Entering Rome after his election at Worms dressed as a humble pilgrim, Leo announced his intent to bring major changes to the Church. He gathered some of the leading reform-minded leaders in the Church and convened an Easter synod in Rome only a few months after his election. At the gathering, the pope directly attacked two severe crises for the Church: simony (the buying and selling of ecclesiastical offices) and the scandal of immorality among the clergy, including concubinage and sodomy. The pope then journeyed across parts of Europe, exhorting bishops to work for reform and encouraging the faithful.

To support the program, one of Leo's closest advisors — the ardent reformer and one-time Benedictine monk, St. Peter Damian — authored a book specifically concerned with sexual misconduct among the clergy. This book, the *Book of Gomorrah*, was first given to Pope Leo probably sometime between 1049 and 1051. Fiery medieval language aside, Peter Damian's book issued concerns and warnings for the Church that were prophetic and timely for every century.

The introduction declared that the primary concern of the Apostolic See must be the "welfare of souls." Because of this, it exhorted the Holy See to proceed against all of those in the Church who were engaged in "a certain abominable and most shameful vice," what was termed "the befouling cancer of sodomy." Damian condemned priests and monks who had violated their vows and engaged in "unclean acts," paying particular attention to those priests who used the confessional to gain access to boys and young men, used the sacrament of penance on their victims, and attempted to rationalize their acts with Church law.

Damian went on to condemn those who were "habituated to the filth of this festering disease" and who in arrogance suggested that they should remain priests or be permitted to seek the priesthood. He urged that any priest guilty of these acts should be removed. Borrowing from St. Paul's letter to the Ephesians (5:5), he asked, " . . . if an unclean man has no inheritance at all in Heaven, how can he be so arrogant as to presume a position of honor in the Church, which is surely the kingdom of God?"

Two other aspects of Damian's book are important. First, he spoke with great clarity about the effects of these acts on both the Church and the victims themselves. Second, he placed the weight of the problem on the shoulders of the bishops and religious superiors. Speaking of the authorities in the Church, he lamented that they all too often were "partners in the guilt of others" through their inaction or willingness to allow the scourge of abuse to continue.

The Council of Trent, the great reforming council in the sixteenth century, took up the issue of clerical abuse in its various deliberations from 1545 to 1563. During its final session, it dealt with the issue of sodomy, even as it detailed reforms in the training and formation of priests. Pope Pius V (1566-1572) augmented this legislation with several decrees against sodomy and abuse by the clergy, among them the constitution *Romani Pontifices*. This decree not only condemned sodomy but also ordered that abusers be removed from their offices and clerical state and remanded to secular authorities for punishment.

Again, the numbers involved have always been tiny as a percentage of the overall population of priests, but Church authorities continued to promulgate revised decrees or instructions as they were deemed necessary. They sometimes focused on specific concerns, such as sodomy or abuses of the confessional. There were, for example, the still relatively obscure instruction from 1922, and the more famous instruction from 1962, both of which dealt with the terrible act of solicitation within confession. The 1922 instruction, issued under Pope Pius XI, was firm in its denunciation of appalling acts by the clergy in the abuse of their sacramental authority. It stipulated among the condemned acts all sexual abuse of children — specifically any child before the age of reason. In 1962, during the pontificate of Pope Blessed John XXIII, an updated Instruction — *Crimen Sollicitationis* — was issued on the same topic, solicitation while hearing confession. What the two instructions reiterated — and what has been lost in many of the discussions and coverage — is that the Church's laws were to be unequivocal. The sexual abuse of minors was seen as a sin as well as a violation of canon law, and it was to be dealt with as a crime.

Nevertheless, the 1922 and 1962 documents have been used repeatedly in the last decade as "smoking guns" against the Church in the quest to prove that Catholic leaders were guilty of mandating "secrecy" at the price of justice and the rights and needs of the victims of terrible abuse by priests. In his interview with the Italian Catholic newspaper *L'Avvenire*, Msgr. Scicluna discussed the issue of secrecy:

A poor English translation of that text has led people to think that the Holy See imposed secrecy in order to hide the facts. But this was not so. Secrecy during the investigative phase served to protect the good name of all the people involved; first and foremost, the victims themselves, then the accused priests who have the right — as everyone does — to the presumption of innocence until proven guilty. The Church does not like showcase justice. Norms on sexual abuse have never been understood as a ban on denouncing the crimes to the civil authorities.

What is manifest from this very brief historical discussion of the Church's opposition to sexual abuse of minors or children in history is that Church authorities have grappled with the problem since the earliest days of the Christian community. It must be stressed that then, as today, the sin and crime of clergy sexual abuse did not occur in large numbers, nor has it been endemic to the institution of the priesthood in the Church. Such is the heinous nature of the act, however, that clergy sexual abuse has been the subject of decrees and canons of councils; the source of worry for saints, theologians, and reforming popes; and a fixture in Church law for many centuries. These offenses are *graviora delicta*, crimes viewed by the Church as the most serious, as well as sacrileges against the faith. The abuse of minors is condemned under the Sixth Commandment and is ranked in gravity with sacrilege against the Eucharist and the violation of the sanctity of the Sacrament of Penance.

Reading the historical background of sexual abuse by some priests and religious, however, should not lead an observer to conclude that the Church has always been corrupt. What the historical record shows is that sexual sins have always been present because they are part of our fallen nature, just as they have long been a part of civil statutes. Aware of this, and sensitive above all to the damage done by a few in the area of sexual abuse of minors, the Church has been determined to resist it and to deal with it both mercifully and justly.

The historical efforts are not the source of shame or failure by an ineffective Church. Rather, they are a testament to the Church's commitment to living as we are called by Christ and to bringing reform and renewal in every age of the world.

CHAPTER FOUR

The Modern Sex Abuse Crisis

*It cannot be denied that some of you [bishops] and your
predecessors failed, at times grievously, to apply the
long-established norms of canon law to the crime of
child abuse.*

— Pope Benedict XVI, Pastoral Letter to the
Catholics of Ireland, March 19, 2010

Two questions can rightly be asked at this point:

- First, if the claim is made that the Church has always
  opposed pedophilia and the abuse of minors, then how
  was it possible that the phenomenon could reach such
  apparently severe dimensions?
- Second, what makes the current abuse crisis different
  from the ones that have troubled the Church in the past?

Several factors all contributed to creating in the modern
clergy sex abuse crisis an atmosphere unmatched by similar challenges of the past. Four reasons are most significant.

First, there was the scale of the crisis. The Church has been
faced with cases of abuse in a host of countries, from Australia to
Poland and from Canada to Brazil. Nowhere, so far, has it been
so well documented as in the United States, where an estimated
4,400 priest abusers have been identified in the past fifty years,
along with 10,667 allegations of abuse.

What are the world numbers? Based on a variety of sur-
veys and studies, the estimate is that in the last fifty years,

between 1.5 and 5 percent of the Catholic clergy has engaged in activity that falls under the heading of sexual abuse of a minor. This seems to hold true both for the United States and for Ireland, where the studies have been most detailed. No organization or society has had this level of scrutiny before, and the statistics — even if small in terms of overall percentage — are both horrifying and overwhelming in terms of sheer numbers involved.

The numbers of priests and victims involved in the United States was documented in the John Jay Report, commissioned by the United States Conference of Catholic Bishops to assess the dimensions of the problem. The report stated that between 1950 and 2002, a total of 10,667 individuals had made allegations of child sexual abuse by 4,392 priests. The number represented 4 percent of the 109,694 priests who had served during those five decades; of the 4,392 priests who were accused, police were contacted regarding 1,021 individuals. Of these, 384 were charged, resulting in 252 convictions and 100 prison sentences. Around 17 percent of accusers had brothers or sisters who were also allegedly abused, and nearly 47 percent of victims claimed to have been abused numerous times.

According to the John Jay Study, 81 percent of the victims were males. The vast majority (78 percent) of the victims were between the ages of 11 and 17; 15 percent of the victims were 16 to 17 years of age; 51 percent were between the ages of 11 and 14. Contrary to the general media image of the abusing priests, only 6 percent of victims were 7 years of age or younger. 16 percent of the victims were between ages 8 and 10. The statistics indicate that most abusers were not technically designated pedophiles (adults or older adolescents who evidence a sexual preference for prepubescent children), but were either *hebephiles* (a sexual preference for pubescent children, approximately between the ages of 10 and 14) or *ephebophiles* (sexual preference of adults for mid-to-late adolescents, between approximately ages 15 and 19).

In total, as of 2009 in the United States, 6 percent of all priests against whom allegations were made were convicted, and about 2 percent received prison sentences. Further details revealed that the majority of incidents of abuse took place in the 1970s, and then declined slowly throughout the 1980s and 1990s. The Jay Report found that the problem was "widespread and affected more than 95 percent of the dioceses and approximately 60 percent of religious communities."

This number is consistent with the same statistics for other religious denominations and in society as a whole. The Crimes Against Children Research Center at the University of New Hampshire reported in 2004 that approximately 200,000 children a year are sexually abused in the United States. And a national report on child sex abuse by educators in public schools prepared for the U.S. Department of Education found that in 2000, 9.6 percent of public school students from kindergarten through eleventh grade reported unwanted sexual harassment or abuse by public school employees; most of the abusers were teachers.

Meanwhile, according to *Insurance Journal*, the insurance companies that insure the majority of Protestant churches in America receive an average of 260 reports each year of young people under 18 being sexually abused by clergy, church staff, volunteers, or congregation members. That number is actually higher than the average of 228 reports each year of "credible accusations" made against Catholic clergy.

Second, there was the way that the crisis became so public. In the past, cases dealt with by Church authorities were often never made public. This was in part a result of confidentiality clauses in some settlement agreements, clauses meant to protect the victim that, in fact, became shields for the guilty as well. Critics often used the confidentiality clauses to argue that "silence" had been procured by buying off the victims or failing to report them to the authorities.

Third, the unwillingness of some civil authorities to prosecute abuse cases (a factor in both the United States and Ireland) made it even less likely that the news would get out or that the Church would be put in an embarrassing situation. In many situations where either the Church was closely aligned with political power (Ireland), or where it felt threatened by a larger Protestant culture that was sometimes quite critical (United States or England), defending the reputation of the Church was a priority.

Fourth, all of this was compounded by the understandable unwillingness of many bishops to believe that such a profound evil could be lurking in parishes, schools, hospitals, and chancery offices — not to mention standing at the altars or sitting in the confessionals of the Catholic Church. As the pope himself has mentioned, some bishops were derelict in their responsibilities to both their people and to their priests; a small number were even guilty of abuse themselves.

The trickle of reports from the mid-1980s on began to expose the issue, but it took on greater momentum first, in 2001, with the release of the Nolan Commission report on abuse cases in England then, in 2002, with the revelation of internal archdiocesan documents in Boston. The Boston documents changed everything — for they showed the world that Church officials in Boston knew about the scandalous behavior of certain predatory priests, and that numerous complaints had been ignored.

This unwelcome exposure of the inner workings of one archdiocese was thanks in part to the work of members of the media, and in part to the victims and their families who were willing to endure the glare of the cameras and the anguish of lawsuits to find justice. Some members of the Catholic clergy, including bishops and cardinals, risked losing friends and advancement by speaking out about the problems in the institutional Church. Public scrutiny and institutional transparency — long shunned by some bishops and religious superiors in the Church — forced the Church to address the issue and begin down the path of redemption and healing. But it came at a high cost.

Peggy Noonan, a Catholic writer and former speechwriter for President Ronald Reagan, asserted in the *Wall Street Journal* (April 2, 2010) that the press deserved gratitude for exposing the scandals and forcing the Church to address its shortcomings:

> All sorts of people have all sorts of motives, but the fact is that the press — the journalistic establishment in the U.S. and Europe — has been the best friend of the Catholic Church on this issue. Let me repeat that: The press has been the best friend of the Catholic Church on the scandals because it exposed the story and made the church face it. The press forced the church to admit, confront and attempt to redress what had happened. The press forced them to confess. The press forced the church to change the old regime and begin to come to terms with the abusers. The church shouldn't be saying *j'accuse* but thank you.

Not all Catholic leaders or Catholic commentators would agree completely with this statement, however. The almost exclusive focus on the sins of the Church — without context or even much curiosity regarding sexual abuse in the wider society — has created the impression that sexual abuse is a "Catholic sin."

The virtual feeding frenzy by journalists eager to convict the pope of insensitivity, collusion, or worse, has only heightened the concern of Catholics that the media is more interested in scalps than the truth. But the Church cannot and should not fear the truth. Archbishop Timothy Dolan of New York, a strong defender of Pope Benedict in the face of the tough coverage and editorial criticism by the *New York Times*, echoed the importance of fair journalism regarding the coverage of the sex abuse scandal. In the same speech in which he criticized the *Times* for its failings and bias, Archbishop Dolan notes:

> The Church needs criticism; we want it; we welcome it; we do a good bit of it ourselves; we do not expect any special treatment . . . so bring it on. All we ask is that it be *fair* and *accurate.*

Finally, related to the failure to prosecute these cases was the institutional breakdown as bishops failed to apply the Church's standing laws and norms.

Deeply wounding for the Church was the notion, which persists to this day, that Church leaders actively conspired to hide abusers, either moving them from assignment to assignment to avoid detection, or worrying more about the reputation of the Church than the damage to the victims. Some bishops did not follow canon law procedures, sought to avoid scandal, and put undue reliance on the psychiatric treatment of offenders — leading critics to conclude that those bishops were acting to hide the criminal behavior. Christopher Hitchens, a self-identified atheist and a harsh critic of the Catholic Church, extended these charges to the pope himself in a commentary on the Webzine Slate.com:

> The supreme leader of the Roman Catholic Church is now a prima facie suspect in a criminal enterprise of the most appalling sort — and in the attempt to obstruct justice that has been part and parcel of that enterprise.

Within the Church, both conservative and liberal critics of the clergy sexual abuse scandal have seen it as a leadership crisis, calling into question the judgment of the men who bore ultimate responsibility for the assignment and care of priests.

Often, bishops and religious superiors listened to the advice of psychiatrists at the time and placed abusive priests into therapy, then reassigned them, in the erroneous belief that they no longer posed a threat to children. The sad truth, however, is that in earlier decades precious few in any profession or segment of society understood the intensity and pervasiveness of the illness that leads to the sexual abuse of minors, and this led to mistakes made by bishops who followed what was considered sound psychiatric and legal advice at the time.

While the psychiatric profession was aware of clinical pedophilia for more than a century, it was mentioned in the *Diagnostic and Statistical Manual* (*DSM*), the primary guide for describing and identifying illnesses, for the first time specifically only in 1952; pedophilia was ranked as a subcategory under the more general classification of "sexual deviation," with no diagnostic criteria provided, suggesting that there were not that many cases. Only in 1980 was pedophilia added to the *DSM* on its own as a primary diagnosis, with diagnostic and therapeutic criteria. Some therapists thought that it was an illness that could be managed or controlled with proper medication and ongoing therapy and encouraged bishops to reassign pedophile priests to ministry. And, though children were sexually abused and pedophilia affected persons in many professions and families, society as a whole did not recognize the problem or discuss it. For this reason, many cases were not reported to the police, and district attorneys declined to prosecute.

In hindsight, these actions and inactions were mistakes made by both Church and civil leaders. Subsequently, in response to the eruption of cases in the last decades, many state legislatures in the United States have changed the law to make reporting of abuse to police compulsory.

As the long effort to eradicate the problem demonstrates, Church authorities were aware of the terrible nature of the sexual abuse of minors. But that awareness lacked the same clinical depth that we have today. Nor were Church officials able to comprehend — as we do today — that this is a societal problem the full dimensions of which we are still trying to comprehend. In his Pastoral Letter to the Catholics of Ireland, Pope Benedict wrote specifically of the failings of the Irish bishops, but his criticism is equally valid for all of the dioceses and archdioceses where the tragedy of abuse, failure and cover-up took place:

> It cannot be denied that some of you and your predecessors failed, at times grievously, to apply the long-established norms of canon law to the crime of child abuse. Serious mistakes were made in responding to allegations. I recognize how difficult it was to grasp the extent and complexity of the problem, to obtain reliable information and to make the right decisions in the light of conflicting expert advice. Nevertheless, it must be admitted that grave errors of judgment were made and failures of leadership occurred. All this has seriously undermined your credibility and effectiveness.

Dr. Thomas Plante — professor and chair of psychology and director of the Spirituality and Health Institute at Santa Clara University and a clinical professor of psychiatry and behavioral sciences at Stanford University School of Medicine — published a study in 2010, *A Perspective on Clergy Sexual Abuse*, in which he found:

First, the available research (which is quite good now) suggests that approximately 4% of priests during the past half century (and mostly in the 1960s and 1970s) have had a sexual experience with a minor (i.e., anyone under the age of 18). There are approximately 60,000 active and inactive priests and brothers in the United States and thus we estimate that between 1,000 and 3,000 priests have sexually engaged with minors. That's a lot. In fact, that is 3,000 people too many. Any sexual abuse of minors whether perpetrated by priests, other clergy, parents, school teachers, boy-scout leaders or anyone else in whom we entrust our children is horrific. However, although good data is hard to acquire, it appears that this 4% figure is consistent with male clergy from other religious traditions and is significantly lower than the general adult male population that is best estimated to be closer to 8%. Therefore, the odds that any random Catholic priest would sexually abuse a minor are not likely to be significantly higher than other males in or out of the clergy. Of course we expect better behavior from priests than from the average man on the street. While even one priest who abuses children is a major problem, we need to keep this issue in perspective and remember that the vast majority of priests do not abuse children. . . .

Almost all the cases coming to light today are cases from 30 and 40 years ago. We did not know much about pedophilia and sexual abuse in general back then. In fact, the vast majority of the research on sexual abuse of minors didn't emerge until the early 1980's. So, it appeared reasonable at the time to treat these men and then return them to their priestly duties. In hindsight, this was a tragic mistake. It has been estimated that 40 years ago about 23% of male psychotherapists have been sexually involved with their clients. Of course this is no longer true today. Forty years ago we thought that autism was caused by cold and withholding mothers referred to as the "ice box mother." We can't take what we know in 2010 and apply it to problems and decisions made in the 1960's and 1970's.

Furthermore, 30 years ago, most priests entered seminary during high school, did not participate in a comprehensive psychological evaluation prior to admission, and had no training in sexuality, maintaining professional boundaries, and impulse control. Advice regarding dealing with sexual impulses included cold showers and prayer. Today, most applicants to the priesthood are much older (generally in their late 20's or 30's). They often have had satisfying and appropriate intimate relationships before entering the seminary. They have completed a psychological evaluation that specifically examines risk factors for sexual problems. They now get good training in sexuality and issues related to managing sexual impulses. It is not surprising that the majority of the sex-offending priests that we hear about in the press are older. In fact, our research indicates that the average age of these men are [sic] 53.

The eruption of the clergy abuse scandal into the American public mind in 2002 brought revelations of sexual crimes and breakdowns in leadership by Church authorities, first in Boston, then across the country. The crisis, however, did not start in Boston in 2002. It began in 1985 when a priest in Louisiana, Gilbert Gauthe, pleaded guilty to eleven counts of molesting boys and was sentenced to prison. The details of the case were described in Jason Berry's book *Lead Us Not into Temptation: Catholic Priests and the Sexual Abuse of Children*. That was followed by the 1992-93 trial of Fr. James Porter of the Fall River diocese, Massachusetts, who was accused and later pled guilty to forty-one counts of abuse of children in five states in the 1960s and 1970s.

A slow rise in reports of clergy abuse of children continued after the initial shock of the Gauthe case. Financial penalties mounted as plaintiffs began to seek not just compensatory damages to cover the cost of counseling, but also punitive damages. The dioceses in the United States were seen as wealthy, with ample insurance coverage; it therefore became increasingly common for plaintiffs' attorneys to make a case that both the abuser and the organization for which he worked were at fault. Failures of supervision, treatment, and notification now became grounds for enormous settlements. Bishops soon discovered that liability insurance carriers for dioceses began to withdraw coverage for actions such as pedophilia or sexual abuse of minors; at times, dioceses had to sue their insurance carriers to cover the costs of settlements.

It was in the shadow of the Porter case that the U.S. bishops first tried to deal with the problem of clergy sexual abuse collectively. Members of what was then the National Conference of Catholic Bishops (now the United States Conference of Catholic Bishops) gathered as a body in South Bend, Indiana, in 1992. During their deliberations, they looked at the growing problem of cases and accusations and approved five principles for handling abuse accusations. The principles demanded:

1. Church officials were to respond immediately to abuse allegations.
2. Priests were to be removed, if evidence supported the allegations, and referred to medical help.
3. All incidents were to be reported, as required by law.
4. The victims of abuse should receive all forms of pastoral, spiritual, and emotional assistance possible.
5. Transparency in dealing with the situation should be embraced, with due respect to the privacy of all involved.

This was an opportunity for many bishops to implement or update policies in their dioceses, as well as to educate the clergy and people about the growing awareness of these issues. Unfortunately, a few bishops chose to add the new principles to the list of unheeded laws and norms — or chose not to implement them, as was their right under Church law. But in those dioceses where these principles and the laws and norms of the Church were followed, cases of abuse were limited and the toxic effects of priestly sexual abuse largely contained.

The next years brought new cases and trials, including the five-year legal odyssey in Dallas over the activities of Fr. Rudolph Kos, culminating in 1998 with the Dallas diocese ordered to pay more than $31 million to Kos' victims (reduced from the original verdict of $119 million). In 1999, one-time Massachusetts priest John Geoghan was indicted on child rape charges. Later dismissed from the clerical state, he was convicted of child abuse and subsequently murdered in prison.

In 2002, the *Boston Globe* won a lawsuit that allowed it access to court records, and therefore documents, of lawsuits settled between the archdiocese of Boston and victims of Geoghan. The documentation from archdiocesan files painted a picture of repeated complaints and warnings about Geoghan, while at the same time he was moved from parish to parish, where he inevitably molested more children. The archdiocese pointed to psychiatric evaluations that said the chances after treatment that he would abuse more children were low — yet he continued to abuse, and complaints continued to be filed.

And the Geoghan trial was just the start of the storm of controversy in the Boston archdiocese, with the scandal coverage driven by the *Boston Globe* newspaper. The names of other accused priests — John Birmingham, Paul Shanley, and Robert Gale — became known across the country. For its reporting on the sex-abuse scandals in Boston, the *Boston Globe* won a Pulitzer Prize. The publication of these documents was a watershed moment for the Church in America.

The archdiocese struggled to pay the legal costs of the cases, and on December 13, 2002, Boston Cardinal Bernard Law — until then one of the most powerful prelates in the United States — resigned. At the time he stepped down, Cardinal Law apologized, saying, "To all those who have suffered from my shortcomings and mistakes I both apologize and from them beg forgiveness."*

Encouraged by the news that priest abusers were being brought to justice, other victims in the archdiocese, across the country, and eventually around the world, came forward and launched a torrent of other accusations and charges and hundreds of millions of dollars in lawsuits. Compounding the scandal was the discovery that bishops, religious orders, and communities had reassigned accused priests to other parishes or schools, thereby permitting the abuse to continue for years. While many bishops had simply followed the recommendations of psychiatrists at the time, the media impression was one of conspiracies and criminal negligence.

The fallout from the scandal in the United States has been monumental. Several bishops have been forced to resign, and the lawsuits stemming from the scandal have cost the Catholic Church in the United States well in excess of $2 billion, with many suits still to be settled or tried. In 2003, the Boston archdiocese agreed to pay $85 million to settle more than 500 civil suits; the archdiocese avoided bankruptcy by agreeing to

---

*He remains the highest-ranking American to resign as a result of the scandal, and even his departure was not without controversy. When Law was named the archpriest of the Basilica of Santa Maria Maggiore in Rome, the media uproar followed him to the Eternal City, as critics of the appointment charged that this was far from a punishment. In 2005, more complaints arose that he should have not been permitted to vote in the conclave following the passing of John Paul II that elected Pope Benedict XVI.

sell land and buildings for more than $100 million to help fund the legal settlements. The California dioceses of Orange, Sacramento, Oakland, and San Diego each settled cases by paying tens of millions of dollars, with Orange paying out a sum of $100 million and San Diego paying $198 million. The largest settlement was made by the archdiocese of Los Angeles. In 2007, Cardinal Roger Mahony agreed to have the archdiocese pay more than $660 million to victims and their lawyers — in addition to $60 million paid out the year before. The deal brought to an end the scheduled trials for a host of abuse claims that dated all the way back to the 1940s.

Several dioceses have been forced into bankruptcy because of the cases, including the archdiocese of Portland and the dioceses of Tucson and Wilmington. The Church's reputation has also been deeply stained, with relentless media attention severely damaging the public esteem of priests and crippling the moral authority of the bishops — even though most had inherited the disaster and were never personally responsible for the mistakes of their predecessors.

CHAPTER FIVE

A Worldwide Scandal

You have suffered grievously and I am truly sorry.
I know that nothing can undo the wrong you have
endured. Your trust has been betrayed and your dignity
has been violated.

— Pope Benedict XVI, Pastoral Letter to the
Catholics of Ireland, March 19, 2010

Within months of the revelations and scandals in the United States becoming part of the national dialogue, the problem of clergy sexual abuse had assumed international dimensions. Victims of abuse, both sexual and physical, began coming forward around the world. Since 2002, the Church in dozens of countries has faced accusations, lawsuits, and intense media scrutiny for failures virtually identical to those documented in the United States. Initially, the crisis was thought to be isolated to a specific part of the Church — such as the English-speaking countries — or limited to places with certain ethnic backgrounds. But this proved to be false, as such varied regions as the Philippines, Hong Kong, the Netherlands, and Italy all were troubled by various cases of abuse. All that changed from area to area were the actual numbers involved and the specifics of the types of abuse found to be present.

The international scope of the scandals tends to overshadow particular damage that has been done to traditionally strong Catholic countries or regions — such as Ireland, Austria, and southern Germany — and the impact on Catholicism in

English-speaking countries, including Australia, Canada, and England. It is useful to focus on several key countries as sad exemplars of the current state of the crisis.

Australia

One of the first countries to suffer from an eruption of controversy was Australia. As in the United States, the bishops of Australia had recognized back in the 1990s that there was a problem. Similarly, solutions they had agreed upon were often either ignored or left unenforced.

The focal point of the abuse claims was in the period after World War II (1939-1945), when the Church willingly took children — nearly 4,000 of them, mostly orphans from Great Britain and Malta — into orphanages and facilities in Western Australia as part of a wider government plan for their relocation.

However, with media scrutiny starting as early as 1967, the system was eventually found to have been inadequate and controversial. Stories began appearing of physical and sexual abuse that took place in some of the facilities, such as the trade schools and orphanages run by the Church's religious communities, including the Christian Brothers. The first reports were followed by books and documentaries on the activities of some members of the religious brothers, problems with the child migration practices, and failures of the government in Australia to provide adequate oversight.

The coverage and growing discussion of abuse in other parts of Australia's Catholic community led the Australian bishops to address the issue as early as 1988. In November of that year, the Australian Catholic Bishops Conference created a "Special Issues Committee" to look at child sexual abuse and to make recommendations for protecting children and handling accusations of misconduct by the clergy. Sadly, years passed before the suggested plan was adopted and implemented, and only in 1992 were the bishops provided with a draft of the protocol.

The following year, the Australian Bishops Conference issued the "Pastoral Statement on Child Protection and Child Sexual Abuse." The bishops acknowledged that there had been incidents of abuse and that failures had taken place in leadership. This was followed by a Statement of Principles in 1994, similar to the five principles adopted by the U.S. bishops in 1992.

By the time the Australian bishops had issued their Statement of Principles, however, Australia was already being rocked by new allegations of abuse by clergy, and trials were convicting Catholic priests and brothers of violence and sexual crimes against children.

Unfortunately, the same thing happened in Australia that had taken place in the United States after its 1992 statement. The bishops adopted the plan, but because it was nonbinding, little action was mandated for dioceses. Some bishops were unwilling to implement the changes; others failed to implement them with vigor; consequently, very little happened to change the long pattern of inactivity. Solving the crisis was pushed down the road, so that when new accusations were made, the bishops seemed negligent in the face of media questions about the earlier prevention plan. And new accusations and new storms did arrive. The end of the twentieth century and beginning of the twenty-first saw trials and convictions of priests and brothers for crimes against children, dating mostly from the 1970s. There were also fresh accusations against priests and religious in dioceses all over Australia; at the start of 2010, seventy-one priests or religious had been convicted of sexual abuse of minors.

Austria

One of the most traditionally Catholic countries in Europe, Austria has been devastated by a series of scandals, reaching from small parishes in the countryside all the way to the office of the Archbishop of Vienna. The result has been the demoralization of Catholic culture and thousands of defections from the Church.

The first major blow came through the resignation in 1995 of the archbishop of Vienna, Cardinal Hermann Gröer. Named archbishop in 1986, Gröer was removed from his office by Pope John Paul II after a flurry of accusations of child sexual abuse that arose concerning the time when Gröer was a teacher at a religious school decades earlier. Soon, other victims came forward, Austrians reacted with outrage, and the archbishop's reputation was destroyed — even though formal charges were never made against him by civil authorities because the statute of limitations had expired.

In February 1998, his successor, Cardinal Christoph Schönborn, declared: "As bishop of this diocese, I apologize for everything by which my predecessor and other church officials have wronged people entrusted to them."

But the Gröer disaster proved only the first of the troubles for the Church in Austria. New scandals began to surface publicly in 2004, when Austrian newspapers published shocking stories about the Seminary of Sankt Pölten diocese — where one of the seminarians had perhaps more than 40,000 photos and films of child pornography and bestiality on his computer. New allegations were soon made of homosexual activity on the part of the priest staff with students. The rector and vice-rector (who was captured in photos kissing a seminarian on the mouth) resigned, followed by Bishop Kurt Krenn, a controversial cleric who headed the diocese and bore ultimate responsibility for the misdeeds. And recently, Bruno Becker, the archabbot of Salzburg's St. Peter's monastery, stepped down amid charges that he had abused a young boy four decades ago.

These revelations of abuse, among others, have exacerbated an already difficult situation and kept the Austrian Church on the defensive.

Canada

While the Catholic population in Canada has never been large, it has enjoyed significant cultural influence in some provinces and cities, most notably in Québec and Montreal. The number of accusations against priests in the country has not been large, either; that being said, they have damaged efforts by Church leaders to increase Catholic presence in an increasingly secularized Canadian culture. Most of the accusations against priests have been centered in the western provinces and in Newfoundland — specifically in its St. John's and Antigonish dioceses.

A series of accusations was made starting in 1988 about criminal sexual activities at Mount Cashel Orphanage in Newfoundland. The Supreme Court of Canada and the Supreme Court of Newfoundland and Labrador have, at various times, ruled that the Church is liable to pay damages for the abuse of children that took place at the hands of Catholic priests. In that light, on August 7, 2009, Bishop Raymond Lahey made the announcement that his diocese of Antigonish had reached a $15 million settlement in a class-action lawsuit filed by victims of diocesan priests, stemming from accusations dating back to the 1950s. However, barely a month later, Bishop Lahey was himself arrested at the Ottawa airport after airport security officials discovered pornographic images of young boys on his laptop computer. Bishop Lahey has resigned, and his case is pending.

Germany

The situation in Germany, as Pope Benedict's home country, has been of particular concern.

The case of Fr. Peter Hullermann, now suspended from active ministry, is only one of many cases that have battered the Catholic Church in Germany and, as in Austria, has demoralized traditional Catholic areas of the country (Bavaria among them).

THE HULLERMANN CONTROVERSY

One clerical abuse case that has most troubled German Catholics, and others around the world, is that of Fr. Peter Hullermann. Hullermann, a priest of the diocese of Essen who transferred to the archdiocese of Munich in 1980, had a record of sexual abuse.

The case in many ways is emblematic of the bureaucratic history of many sexual abuse cases. Hullermann was allowed to enter the Munich archdiocese for therapy at the request of Fr. Klaus Malangré of the Essen diocese — following the prevailing perception of the time that sexual problems could be addressed by a combination of therapy and spiritual repentance and renewal.

According to documents reported on by the *Times*, Cardinal Ratzinger was informed on January 15, 1980, "that a priest from Essen in need of psychiatric treatment required room and board in a Munich Congregation. 'The request is granted,' read the minutes, stipulating that Father Hullermann would live at St. John the Baptist Church." Fr. Hullermann arrived in February, and according to a subsequent memo, assumed some clerical duties almost immediately after beginning his psychiatric treatment.

According to the archdiocese of Munich, Cardinal Ratzinger did not know of the subsequent decision — apparently approved by his Vicar General, Msgr. Gerhard Gruber — to allow for Fr. Hullermann's employment in the archdiocese. So, although the *New York Times* has reported that the cardinal was copied on a memo to this effect, there is no evidence that the cardinal himself ever reviewed it. What is known is that subsequently Fr. Hullermann was allowed to remain in the archdiocese and to practice as a priest.

What is also known is that in 1986 — long after Cardinal Ratzinger had left for Rome — Fr. Hullermann was convicted of child sexual abuse by German authorities and given an eighteen-month suspended sentence and a fine. He remained a practicing priest in the archdiocese until the controversy exploded in 2010, when he was suspended from the priesthood for violating a rule that he not associate with children. His supervisor, Fr. Josef Obermaier, has resigned, and the Archbishop of Munich from 1981 to 2007, Cardinal Friedrich Wetter, has apologized.

On March 26, 2010, the archdiocese of Munich and Freising issued the following statement regarding the *New York Times* article and then-Cardinal Ratzinger:

> The article in the *New York Times* contains no additional information to that which the archdiocese has already made public concerning the status of the former Archbishop's knowledge of the personal file. The archdiocese remains convinced that the former Archbishop was unaware of the decision to employ the priest H[ullerman] for pastoral care in a parish and repudiates as pure speculation any other representation of the matter. The Vicar-General of that time, Prelate Gerhard Gruber, has assumed full responsibility for his unauthorized and erroneous decision to employ H. in pastoral care in a parish.

While the case exemplifies the mishandling of pedophilia cases that have plagued many dioceses, then-Cardinal Ratzinger is known only to have approved the transfer of the priest seeking psychiatric treatment for issues of a sexual nature.

The cases are consistent with those found elsewhere, with priests (and several nuns) facing accusations of abuse and misconduct dating back to the 1970s and 1980s and extending across all of Germany. To date, at least eighteen of Germany's twenty-seven dioceses have cases or allegations under investigation, and more than 400 allegations of sexual abuse have been made. Responding to public outcry, the German Minister of Justice, Sabine Leutheusser-Schnarrenberger, announced her intention to launch a full investigation into how the Church's leaders have dealt with the accusations in the past, alleging that there has been a "wall of silence" around the issue. Archbishop Robert Zollitsch of Freiburg, president of the German Bishops Conference, apologized in February for sexual abuse of children by Catholic priests — even as he admitted that he had failed to report abusive priests to state authorities after disciplining them. In January 2010, former students at Berlin's prestigious Jesuit high school, Canisius College, made public their accusations against two former priests at the institution. This was followed in early March by the revelation that young singers in the famed Regensburger Domspatzen choir — which Monsignor Georg Ratzinger (the pope's older brother) had directed from 1964 to 1994 — endured sexual abuse and beatings by some priests and seminarians since the 1950s. Msgr. Ratzinger, who is long retired, denied any knowledge of sexual abuse during his time as head of the choir. He has admitted to having slapped several of the singers, as part of the then-accepted form of discipline. But he also apologized for having done little to alleviate the beatings and welcomed the 1980 ban on corporal punishments.

Ireland

With the possible exception of the United States, the sex abuse scandal has had no greater impact and has received no wider media attention than in Ireland. A nation literally formed and nurtured by the Catholic faith in the face of persecution, injustice, hardship, oppression, and even mass. starvation, Ireland has long been a model of the idealized "Catholic country." As Pope Benedict lauded it in his Pastoral Letter to the Catholics of Ireland:

> Historically, the Catholics of Ireland have proved an enormous force for good at home and abroad. Celtic monks like Saint Columbanus spread the Gospel in Western Europe and laid the foundations of medieval monastic culture. The ideals of holiness, charity and transcendent wisdom born of the Christian faith found expression in the building of churches and monasteries and the establishment of schools, libraries and hospitals, all of which helped to consolidate the spiritual identity of Europe. Those Irish missionaries drew their strength and inspiration from the firm faith, strong leadership and upright morals of the Church in their native land. . . . From the sixteenth century on, Catholics in Ireland endured a long period of persecution, during which they struggled to keep the flame of faith alive in dangerous and difficult circumstances. . . . In almost every family in Ireland, there has been someone — a son or a daughter, an aunt or an uncle — who has given his or her life to the Church. Irish families rightly esteem and cherish their loved ones who have dedicated their lives to Christ, sharing the gift of faith with others, and putting that faith into action in loving service of God and neighbor.

Given this extraordinary history, no nation has been harder hit than Ireland by the staggering dimensions of the scandal in the last decade. The investigations by the press, the government, and the Church have revealed failures at virtually every level of ecclesiastical and civil oversight and protection.

Other countries with sex abuse cases have been able to make the proper claim that the number of abusive priests was relatively low; there was no institutional problem of abuse and violence. But what has set Ireland apart is the degree to which the unimaginable abuse of children took place in the so-called "industrial schools" that were entrusted to the Church to run. A kind of systemic pattern of abuse occurred in many of the schools, and Church and government leaders failed to stop it.

So widely known were these reports of abuse that in 1946, Fr. Edward J. Flanagan, the famed founder of Boy's Town in the United States, went to Ireland to investigate the stories and speak out against the abuses. According to Thomas Craughwell, writing in *Our Sunday Visitor*, Father Flanagan called the brutal methods used in the schools "a disgrace to the nation" and "a scandal, un-Christlike and wrong." Irish politicians rejected Fr. Flanagan's criticisms, however, and no reforms were instituted.

Over the last few decades, the Irish Church faced a large number of cases of pedophile and abusive priests. But few, if any, Catholics were prepared for the findings released in two reports in May and November 2009, respectively. The first was by the Commission to Inquire into Child Abuse — the so-called Ryan Report, after the commission's chair, Justice Sean Ryan. The second was the government inquiry into abuse in the archdiocese of Dublin from 1975 to 2004 — the Murphy Report, named after Judge Yvonne Murphy, the commission head.

The five-volume Ryan Report — the result of a nine-year, $70 million investigation — spelled out in stark and unrelentingly objective terms the six decades of physical, sexual, and psychological horrors inflicted on children in Ireland's residential institutions run by fifteen religious orders. The Irish people knew what was coming in the Ryan Report, but the actual documentation revealed a scale of evil and suffering thought unimaginable. As Austen Ivereigh wrote in *Our Sunday Visitor*'s coverage of the report:

Apart from a few lone voices, leaders in the Church and the state routinely looked away from what was happening. It is hard to know which is the more painful to read: the rapes and the beatings, the emotional detachment of the religious brothers and sisters, or the failure by government inspectors to do anything about it.

The Murphy Report, meanwhile, narrowed the focus from the country's industrial schools to the archdiocese of Dublin. What it found was a systematic willingness on the part of Catholic leaders to ignore terrible cases of abuse and sexual misconduct — in the hope, mainly, of protecting the good name of the Church. The report documented that four different Dublin archbishops refused to deal with the abuse problem for nearly three decades, from 1975 to 2004.

Few Irish bishops escaped some degree of involvement, and as a result of the fallout, four bishops resigned. Even the primate of all Ireland, Cardinal Sean Brady of Armagh, was implicated when it was learned in March 2010 that he had been present as a young priest at meetings in 1975 at which children had signed vows of silence regarding a case against a pedophile priest. Cardinal Brady issued a complete apology, but calls mounted for him to resign.

In the aftermath of the Murphy Report, Archbishop Martin of Dublin, speaking to the Irish people, issued an apology on behalf of the Catholic Church in Ireland:

> As Archbishop of a diocese for which I have pastoral responsibility, of my own native diocese, of the diocese for which I was ordained a priest, of a diocese which I love and hope to serve to the best of my ability, what can I say when I have to share with you the revolting story of the sexual assault and rape of so many young children and teenagers by priests of the archdiocese or

who ministered in the diocese? No words of apology will ever be sufficient. . . .

The sexual abuse of a child is and always was a crime in civil law; it is and always was a crime [in] canon law; it is and always was grievously sinful.

One of the most heartbreaking aspects of the Report is that while Church leaders — Bishops and religious superiors — failed, almost every parent who came to the diocese to report abuse clearly understood the awfulness of what has involved. Almost exclusively their primary motivation was to try to ensure that what happened to their child, or in some case to themselves, did not happen to other children. Their motivation was not about money or revenge; it was quite simply about that most basic human sense of right and wrong and that basic Christian motivation of concern for others. The survivors of abuse who courageously remained determined to have the full truth heard by all deserve our recognition and admiration. . . .

How did those with responsibility dramatically misread the risk that a priest who had hurt one of those whom Jesus calls "the little ones" might go on to abuse another child if decisive action was not taken? Excuses, denials, and minimizations were taken from priest abusers who were at the least in denial, at worst devious in multiple ways, and decisions were taken which resulted in more children being abused. Efforts made to "protect the Church" and to "avoid scandal" have had the ironic result of bringing this horrendous scandal on the Church today.

The damage done to children abused by priests can never be undone. As Archbishop of Dublin and as Diarmuid Martin — a person — I offer to each and every survivor, my apology, my sorrow and my shame for what happened to them. I am aware, however, that no words of apology will ever be sufficient. . . .

PART THREE

Benedict XVI and the Road to Renewal

CHAPTER SIX

"Where Do We Go from Here?"

We will absolutely exclude pedophiles from the sacred ministry; it is absolutely incompatible, and whoever is really guilty of being a pedophile cannot be a priest.
— Pope Benedict XVI, in-flight press conference on his way to the United States, April 15, 2008

In his homily at the Chrism Mass in 2010, Dublin's Archbishop Martin asked the sensible question: "Where do we go from here?" As the Church in Ireland and many other parts of the world struggles with the revelation of sexual abuse cases among their own clergy, they may find that the way forward out of this crisis has been blazed by the United States Church, itself so wracked by scandals only years before.

"Where do we go from here" was the question asked by the bishops of the United States when they met in Dallas in June 2002. Under an avalanche of cases and lawsuits and the firestorm of media reporting on failings and cover-ups, they understood that the 1992 directives were not enough. The principles had lacked any enforcement mechanisms; individual bishops had failed to meet the requirements and norms of Church law; and the bishops had not pursued an investigation into the root causes of the crisis.

The archbishops and bishops on the front line of the crisis in those dioceses beset by lawsuits and new revelations had the immediate task of repairing the breach of trust that had occurred with the Catholics in the pews, even as they struggled with the canonical, legal, and financial implications of the many cases now inundating them. Several bishops would retire or step down in the year following the scandal, and the financial toll mounted quickly, soon to impact severely the functioning of many dioceses.

And, from the start of the meeting, the bishops were on the defensive under a wave of media attention and criticism. The tone of the 800 journalists covering the event was captured by a joking reference made by some to the path the bishops took to get to their meeting hall each morning. It was called "the perp walk" — "perp" being slang for criminal perpetrators. Overlooked in many media reports was that the bishops chose to have two victims of clergy sexual abuse speak candidly and movingly to the assembled body of bishops about their experiences.

In this media fishbowl, there was no question that the leadership of the Church in the United States and in the Vatican recognized the gravity of the situation and the need to impose effective norms. Out of this meeting of bishops came what has come to be known as the Dallas Charter (*Charter for the Protection of Children and Young People*). The Charter made clear that the bishops themselves saw the abuse crisis as primarily a problem involving priests, and the focus of the charter was guidelines for priests and Church employees.

Key provisions of the charter include:

- The establishment of the National Review Board and the Office of Child and Youth Protection.
- The "Essential Norms for Diocesan/Eparchial Policies Dealing With Allegations of Sexual Abuse of Minors by Priests or Deacons," which established legal procedures under church law for applying charter policies.
- Encouraging bishops or their representatives to meet with victims.

- Establishing offices to receive accusations and to provide professional counseling to victims.
- Setting up diocesan review boards to examine accusations and advise the bishop on policies.
- Permanently removing a priest or deacon from ministry after he admits committing abuse or his guilt is established after an appropriate Church process, commonly referred to as "zero tolerance."
- Prohibiting confidentiality clauses in settlements with victims, unless requested by the victim.
- Improving seminary training and providing ongoing priestly formation programs to strengthen the commitment to celibacy.

The newly created National Review Board was then asked to commission a thorough study on the full dimensions of the phenomenon and scope of clergy sexual abuse in the United States. What resulted was a study undertaken by the John Jay College of Criminal Justice — officially titled *The Nature and Scope of the Problem of Sexual Abuse of Minors by Catholic Priests and Deacons in the United States* — known more generally as the John Jay Report. Completed in 2004, it covered the period from 1950 to 2002.

This study remains the single most significant effort to document all of the relevant details of the sex abuse problem and has since served as the basic template for other national churches in their own investigations. It is also one of the very few comprehensive studies of its type undertaken by any organization, and perhaps the most thorough. (The "causes and contexts" companion study is scheduled for completion in 2010.)

The Charter and its related documents were controversial because of their mandates upon bishops, which some considered an infringement upon the rights of episcopal authority in the Church. Still, the U.S. bishops in attendance recognized the need for a more effective response than had been given to that point; at the conclusion of their discussions, they approved the *Charter for the Protection of Children and Young People* by a vote of 239 to 13.

Some bishops, deeming the mandates unnecessary in their dioceses, did not approve the Charter nor submit to its mandates. One of them, Bishop Fabian Bruskewitz of the diocese of Lincoln (Nebraska), refused to sign the Charter; his reason was, as he stated, that his diocese was already in full compliance with both Church and all civil laws. He has subsequently not participated in the audits by the National Review Board, which is his right as a bishop under Church law.

Although many people think of the Church in terms of a multinational corporation, with the Vatican as the home office and each diocese as a branch (with each parish as a kind of smaller office), in fact, the Church is structured as a government and not a corporation. The relationship between a diocese and the Vatican is best characterized as the relationship between a state and the federal government. Each diocese is a complete local church; instead of being thought of as a division of the universal Church (a top-down approach), a diocese is considered a constitutive cell of the universal Church (a more organic approach that recognizes that the universal Church is built up from the many local churches that comprise it). Akin to the relationship between state and federal governments in the United States, in the Church, the local bishop possesses great autonomy and freedom to govern according to local needs and priorities. As Peter was to the other Apostles, so the successor of Peter acts in the universal Church — to build up and support the communion of the Church worldwide, not to govern it with strict authority. Vatican II spoke rather poignantly of this in several documents, stressing the collegiality of bishops in union with their head, rather than the top-down authority of the Roman Pontiff over other bishops.

The Vatican monitored closely the events in Dallas in 2002 and met with the American bishops to clarify and assist their work. In April 2002, Pope John Paul convened a gathering of the American Cardinals, the heads of the U.S. bishops' conference, and Cardinal Ratzinger and other Vatican officials, in Rome. At the time, he declared forcefully that there was "no place in the priesthood and religious life for those who would harm the young" — although he added that it was important to remember "the power of Christian conversion."

The primary focus of the Charter, therefore, was to create clear and enforceable parameters for every diocese and Catholic institution that would guarantee a "safe environment" for all children and young people who might have any kind of contact with the Church or take part in any activities sponsored by the Church. This entailed the strict enforcement of a "zero tolerance" policy for sexual abuse and sexual abusers, along with uniform national procedures for the investigation of sex-abuse allegations against all personnel working for and serving the Church, including lay teachers in Catholic schools, parish staff, coaches, and all other volunteers assisting the Church in the care of young people. Oversight entailed background checks for Church employees and training in creating and sustaining a safe environment for youth, as well as in recognizing and reporting potential abuse.

At the same time, to guarantee that every diocese in the country would follow the same procedures and regulations in handling abuse allegations, on June 14, 2002, the bishops approved the "Essential Norms for Diocesan/Eparchial Policies Dealing with Allegations of Sexual Abuse of Minors by Priest or Deacons." The bishops then sent the Essential Norms to Rome for required approval — or *recognitio* — by the Holy See.

This procedure was required because, while a national bishops' conference does possess authority to enact legislation where granted it by the Church's universal law, this was not one of those situations. The Essential Norms represented an imposition of regulations and laws on the dioceses of the United States, and thus needed to be examined for any possible conflicts with wider law that governs the universal Church. The Essential Norms, governing a part of the universal Church, are called particular law. As such, they needed approval by the Holy See.

To assist this process, a delegation of bishops met in Rome with officials of the relevant offices of the Roman Curia (central offices of the Holy See), including the Congregation for the Doctrine of the Faith, in October 2002. After minor changes were made, the *recognitio* from the Holy See was given on December 8, 2002, and the norms were accepted as particular law for all of the dioceses of the United States, effective March 1, 2003. They were accepted as complementary to the universal law of the Church, which already stipulated penalties for the grave sins and acts of sexual abuse against minors. The bishops re-approved the set of norms in 2006.

For the Church in the United States, the Charter and the Essential Norms were a vital starting point toward reconciliation and renewal. A shield had been installed for dioceses, and there was at last an enforceable set of norms particularly aimed at the laws and needs of the Catholic community in the United States. This was, as many bishops readily acknowledged, only a start.

Has progress been made since 2002? In truth, immense progress has been made in three key areas that were considered vital in the Charter: creating a safe environment and preventing further abuse, improving the seminaries and priestly formation, and promoting genuine healing for the victims. In the midst of the current controversy, the U.S. bishops' conference released the results of the 2009 annual report on compliance with the *Charter for the Protection of Children and Young People* in March 2010. The report was a striking testimony to the success of the Essential Norms, the work of the bishops, and the achievement of Benedict XVI in bringing genuine hope for the future regarding the tragedy of sex abuse by the clergy. The numbers revealed the fewest number of victims, allegations, and offenders in dioceses since 2004, and most of the cases reported to dioceses were from decades ago.

In 2009, there were 398 allegations and 286 offenders reported to dioceses. Of the allegations reported in 2009, a grand total of six allegations (or a mere 2 percent) involving children under the age of 18 took place in 2009 — out of a priestly population of nearly 42,000 and a Catholic population of nearly 70 million.

Approximately one-eighth of the allegations reported in 2009 (forty-eight in all) were unsubstantiated or determined to be false. Similar results were reported for members of the religious orders of men. The majority of new allegations (71 percent) involved cases in which the abuse took place between 1960 and 1984, with most occurring between 1975 and 1979. As a result of these declines, there was a one-year decline of 83 percent in the amounts paid out for settlements from the previous year. Dioceses also paid more than $21 million to continue their efforts in child protection, such as training programs, background checks, and salaries for staff. Nearly six million, or 96 percent, of children in Catholic schools or religious education programs had received Safe Environment training. Background evaluations were also performed on over two million priests, deacons, seminarians, educators, employees, and volunteers.

In a memo to all bishops, Cardinal Francis George, president of the U.S. Conference of Catholic Bishops, wrote:

> The number of children now equipped with the skills to protect themselves more effectively continues to grow. The *Charter* is causing a cultural change in the U.S. Catholic Church, one I hope will permeate all areas of society. Of course, as bishops, we take the responsibility to reach out to victims/survivors and create safe environments seriously. The life and dignity of the victims/survivors and of little ones lie at the core of our responsibilities as shepherds.

As quickly and thoroughly as the media descended on the Church when the abuse crisis surfaced, however, coverage of the efforts to address and remedy the situation in the Church has not been nearly as thorough. In his blog on the archdiocesan Web site, New York's Archbishop Dolan expressed his frustration at that disparity:

> We Catholics have for a decade apologized, cried, reached out, shouted *mea culpa,* and engaged in a comprehensive reform that has met with widespread acclaim. We've got a long way to go, and the reform still has to continue.
>
> But it is fair to say that, just as the Catholic Church may have been a bleak example of how *not* to respond to this tragedy in the past, the Church is now a model of *what to do.* As the *National Review Online* observes, ". . . the Church's efforts to come to grips with this problem within the household of faith — more far reaching than in any other institution or sector of society — have led others to look to the Catholic Church for guidance on how to address what is, in fact, a global plague."

As another doctor, Paul McHugh, an international scholar on this subject at Johns Hopkins University, remarked, "Nobody is doing more to address the tragedy of sexual abuse of minors than the Catholic Church."

During his 2008 visit to the United States, Pope Benedict XVI spoke to the U.S. bishops about their efforts to create a safe environment and their ramifications for the society at large:

> If they are to achieve their full purpose . . . the policies and programs you have adopted need to be placed in a wider context. . . . All have a part to play in this task — not only parents, religious leaders, teachers and catechists, but the media and entertainment industries as well. Indeed, every member of society can contribute to this moral renewal and benefit from it.

One of the other areas that became manifestly obvious in the studies related to the roots of the crisis was that of deficiencies in the formation and training of seminarians. Here, too, Pope Benedict has provided vital leadership.

In 2002, during the visit of the American bishops and the officials of the Holy See, the proposal was made to conduct a thorough visitation of the seminary system in the United States. Pope Benedict approved the investigation in 2005 and appointed Archbishop Edwin O'Brien to coordinate it.

In a 2006 talk at the Catholic Press Association Convention in Nashville, Tennessee, Archbishop O'Brien, as quoted by Catholic News Service, said that:

> . . . the objectives of the visitations, which were sparked by the sexual abuse crisis that hit the U.S. church in 2002, were to examine the criteria for admission of candidates and various aspects of priestly formation, including the intellectual formation of seminarians in the field of moral theology and the programs of human and spiri-

tual formation aimed at ensuring they can faithfully live chaste, celibate lives.

The actual visitation took place between September 2005 and July 2006 and consisted of 117 bishops and seminary personnel formed into small teams. They visited 156 diocesan and religious seminaries and houses of formation.

"During the visits, the teams interviewed seminarians, faculty, staff and members of the board of directors," Archbishop O'Brien said. He added that there were ten areas of concentration, including the concept of the priesthood, governance of the seminary, admission policies, academic formation, human formation, pastoral formation, and service of the seminary to the newly ordained. He went on to explain that there were a total of fifty-six questions, out of which six required answers:

> These had to do with whether psychological testing was employed in admissions procedures; if the interviewee had concerns about the moral life of the seminary; whether there was evidence of homosexuality in the seminary; whether there was adequate formation to enable seminarians to live a life of celibacy and chastity; whether students were being prepared to respond to the moral relativism they would face in the society; and whether the seminary checked regularly for impediments to ordination.

A report was later released by Vatican authorities that pointed to ways that the seminaries might be improved in the areas of the priestly identity, the governance of the schools (including a concern about the lack of enforcement of the provisions for removing faculty members who dissent from Church teaching), criteria for the proper admission and suitability of candidates, and the proper formation of seminarians. Pope Benedict discussed the importance of this oversight for the renewal of seminary formation during his 2008 visit to the United States:

> We have made a visitation of the seminaries and we will do all that is possible in the education of seminarians for a deep spiritual, human and intellectual formation for the students. Only sound persons can be admitted to the priesthood and only persons with a deep personal life in Christ and who have a deep sacramental life.

Meanwhile, during the same visit, the pope spoke repeatedly about the need for healing and pastoral outreach to victims of abuse. During his address to the American bishops in 2008, Pope Benedict reminded them of their obligations to the victims:

> As you strive to eliminate this evil wherever it occurs, you may be assured of the prayerful support of God's people throughout the world. Rightly, you attach priority to showing compassion and care to the victims. It is your God-given responsibility as pastors to bind up the wounds caused by every breach of trust, to foster healing, to promote reconciliation and to reach out with loving concern to those so seriously wronged.

In an editorial appearing on Easter Sunday, 2010, in the *Washington Post*, Archbishop Donald Wuerl of the Washington archdiocese wrote in defense of the pontiff and answered the question of what role Pope Benedict has played in this process of reform and reconciliation:

> This commitment to safety has been done with the support and leadership of Pope Benedict XVI.
> Then-Cardinal Ratzinger, as the head of the Congregation for the Doctrine of the Faith, and Pope John Paul II were strong voices supporting the American bishops when we asked for changes in canon law and for spe-

cial norms to expedite the removal of priests involved in sexual abuse of minors in a quick and decisive manner.

Pope Benedict has made pastoral care a priority. Two years ago this month, he stood with us at Mass at Nationals Park and spoke about the sexual abuse of minors: "No words of mine could describe the pain and harm inflicted by such abuse. It is important that those who have suffered be given loving pastoral attention. Nor can I adequately describe the damage that has occurred within the community of the Church."

One of the most poignant moments of the Holy Father's visit to our city was his private visit with victims of clergy sexual abuse. He spoke with each person, he listened to them, he prayed with them and he heard how devastating the abuse was to their lives.

CHAPTER SEVEN

The Way Forward

Victims should receive compassion and care, and those responsible for these evils must be brought to justice.

— Pope Benedict XVI, Mass in Sydney, Australia,
July 19, 2008

European Catholicism stands today where the Catholic community in the United States found itself nearly a decade ago. The authority, integrity, credibility, and competence of the bishops seem to be in tatters. Dedicated and faithful priests and religious are humiliated and angry, feeling betrayed by some of their peers and, at times, distant from their own bishops. The lay faithful are angry, shocked, and frustrated. And the many victims feel either ignored or attacked by Church authorities.

Much as some American Catholics felt the temptation to walk away, to throw up their hands and abandon the Church, so, too, many European Catholics have found it difficult to conceive a way for the Church to recover from this disaster. Persisting in hope becomes even more difficult with each new day bringing fresh revelations and new cases of abuse or failure.

On March 13, 2010, Vatican spokesman Fr. Federico Lombardi appeared on Vatican Radio and discussed the controversy surrounding the Church in Europe and Pope Benedict XVI. At that time, he stated that the way forward is before us:

> Despite the tempest, the Church clearly sees the path to follow, under the certain and rigorous leadership of the

Holy Father. As we have already observed, we hope that in the end this travail can be a help to society as a whole to take ever better care of the protection and formation of children and youth.

There is a way forward, and the actions of the Church in the United States gives part of the signpost for the future. As in the United States, the Church in Europe must look at the underlying causes of the crisis and the reforms that will be necessary to bring about the renewal of their churches.

The pope articulated some of these issues in his Pastoral Letter to the Catholics of Ireland:

> Only by examining carefully the many elements that gave rise to the present crisis can a clear-sighted diagnosis of its causes be undertaken and effective remedies be found. Certainly, among the contributing factors we can include: inadequate procedures for determining the suitability of candidates for the priesthood and the religious life; insufficient human, moral, intellectual and spiritual formation in seminaries and novitiates; a tendency in society to favor the clergy and other authority figures; and a misplaced concern for the reputation of the Church and the avoidance of scandal, resulting in failure to apply existing canonical penalties and to safeguard the dignity of every person. Urgent action is needed to address these factors, which have had such tragic consequences in the lives of victims and their families, and have obscured the light of the Gospel to a degree that not even centuries of persecution succeeded in doing.

European Church leaders are already beginning to take to heart some of the hard lessons of the crisis: admitting the failures on the part of Church leaders, working for healing for the victims and their families, restoring the confidence and credibility for Church leadership, and rooting out the priest offenders to safeguard against future misconduct. What becomes apparent in this process of reform and renewal is how crucial Pope Benedict XVI has been in shaping it and giving it such clear direction.

It is too early to state with total confidence that the initial measures will correct all of the problems, or that they are yet adequate at achieving the healing and redemption needed for a true renewal of European Catholicism. But they are a crucial start for the specific needs and particular laws of European dioceses, while echoing the steps taken successfully in the United States.

One place where this template is already in place is in the United Kingdom. England and Wales have not escaped the plague of sexual abuse, with cases centering especially in the diocese of Arundel, the archdiocese of Cardiff, and the English Benedictines. In July 2000, the public was also shocked to learn that the then recently appointed Archbishop of Westminster, Archbishop (later Cardinal) Cormac Murphy-O'Connor, had allowed a pedophile priest to remain in ministry in the 1980s, when he was bishop of Arundel and Brighton. The archbishop acknowledged his mistakes and apologized; then, he took steps to prevent a second occurrence on his "watch" — or that of any other bishop in the United Kingdom.

In September 2000, Archbishop Murphy-O'Connor formed an independent committee to be chaired by Lord Nolan, a Catholic life peer and Law Lord, to examine the Church's policy on child protection. This panel, comprised of police, psychiatrists, and various other experts, presented the results of their review in 2001, under the title *A Program for Action* — known generally as the Nolan Report. While some questions were raised as to whether its provisions adhered properly to canon law, the Nolan Report assisted the bishops of the United Kingdom in the creation of the Catholic Office for the Protection of Children and Vulnerable Adults (COPCA) and provided direction for mechanisms for enforcement of a firm policy in all dioceses throughout England and Wales. European bishops have also been quick to reach out to the victims of sexual abuse and their families. Cardinal Christoph Schönborn of Vienna — who inherited the scandal of Cardinal Hermann Gröer, the seminary of Sankt Pölten, and the abuse cases across the archdiocese of Vienna — has emerged as a key figure in reforming the Austrian Church. He has spoken about the need for the Church to make an "unflinching examination" as to the causes of the scandal. He also held a "day of repentance" service — part of "an acknowledgement of guilt in the name of the Church" — in Vienna's St. Stephen's Cathedral in March 2010.

The event included Mass, a formal apology by the archbishop of Austria's largest archdiocese, and statements by victims of clerical abuse. Cardinal Schönborn thanked Austrian victims for breaking their silence, while acknowledging that there is still much to be done. He has announced his intention to name a Church-funded but independent commission to strengthen the guidelines for dealing with clergy sexual abuse. A hotline has also been set up for victims of violence and sexual abuse by Catholic Church clergy to call and report incidents.

In Switzerland, the bishops announced the creation of an independent commission to investigate abuse claims and admitted that they had underestimated the problem. Not only did they urge victims to consider filing criminal complaints with authorities; they also called on all those guilty of abuse to stand before God and the people whom they have wronged and turn themselves into the relevant authorities. (Under Swiss law, the clergy are not currently required to report sexual abuse cases to civil authorities.)

In Germany, one of the current epicenters of the

controversy, the German bishops' conference issued an apology in February 2010:

> Revelations of sexual abuse against minors by clerics and church staff have shaken us in recent days. We bishops stand up to our responsibility. We condemn the crimes committed by the members of religious orders as well as by priests and staff of our dioceses. Shamed and shocked, we apologize sincerely to all those who have become victims of these despicable deeds and beg their forgiveness.

The bishops committed themselves to "get to the roots of each case and inform the public openly and honestly, free from false considerations, even when incidents are reported to us that lie far in the past. The victims have a right to this."

On March 12 — following a meeting between Pope Benedict and a group of leading German bishops at the Vatican, at which the pope encouraged the German bishops to act "with decision and courage" — Archbishop Robert Zollitsch of Freiburg, the head of the German bishops' conference, told reporters that the Church in Germany was committed to admitting the truth and helping the victims, collaborating and cooperating with all ecclesiastical and civil authorities, and formulating a comprehensive set of guidelines for cases, the care of victims, and the creation of a "culture of prevention," with guidelines for schools and Church-related activities where children are present.

One area of concern for observers is the potential complication that can ensue because, under German law, Church authorities are not required to report cases to law enforcement. The bishops announced that they would revise those requirements for German dioceses over the next months, and the bishops of the German region of Bavaria also stated that there should be a system of automatic reporting of cases.

These efforts drew the praise of German Chancellor Angela Merkel.

In Ireland, home to arguably the worst national scandal because of the sheer scale, the Irish bishops have responded in various ways since the shock of the Ryan and Murphy Reports. Some have resigned, including Bishop John Magee — the one-time secretary to Popes Paul VI, John Paul I, and John Paul II — who had become bishop of Cloyne in 1987. He was found to have known about accusations against two priests in 1995 but failed to report them to civil authorities until 2003. Having already been removed from diocesan administration in 2009, he resigned officially on March 24, 2010, after making a formal apology:

> As I depart, I want to offer once again my sincere apologies to any person who has been abused by any priest of the diocese of Cloyne during my time as bishop or at any time. To those whom I have failed in any way, or through any omission of mine have made suffer, I beg forgiveness and pardon.

In February 2010, in the wake of the official reports, the pope summoned all active Irish bishops to Rome for an unprecedented summit to discuss the situation, demand an explanation from them, and coordinate steps for reform. The two days of meetings ended with a Vatican communiqué that indicated the Irish bishops to be undertaking a series of steps to deal with the immense challenges ahead:

> The Bishops likewise described the support at present being provided by thousands of trained and dedicated lay volunteers at parish level to ensure the safety of children in all Church activities, and stressed that, while there is no doubt that errors of judgment and omissions stand at the heart of the crisis, significant measures have now been

taken to ensure the safety of children and young people. They also emphasized their commitment to cooperation with the statutory authorities in Ireland — North and South — and with the National Board for Safeguarding Children in the Catholic Church in Ireland to guarantee that the Church's standards, policies, and procedures represent best practice in this area.

Cardinal Sean Brady, archbishop of Armagh and primate of all Ireland (a prelate under intense pressure because of his admission of mistakes in the past), was frank in his recognition that recovery for the Church could not have a timetable attached to it. He added, however:

> [W]e will make every possible effort to heal this wound and also with the help of God we will succeed. Collaborating with the state and with all the faithful who are helping us in this service. It is very important for the future of the Church, because the boys and youths are the future of the Church.

Even as the cases grew in number in the United States and around the world, the Holy See was not inactive in watching and assessing the best ways to deal with the problem. Sadly, the system of oversight envisioned by the Church — as stated in canon law and the documents such as those promulgated by the Holy See in 1922 and 1962 concerning abuses within the context of the confessional — were thwarted by many bishops' failure to comply with existing provisions of canon law. Additional discrepancies included the ways various national churches dealt with abuse cases under differing legal systems and requirements around the world. The bishops' conferences now recognize these obstacles. As a result, bishops in various countries have created independent consultative bodies, at both national and diocesan levels, to assess every case and monitor bishops' responses to accusations. This is also the reason some conferences have commissioned outside, third-party annual reviews of each diocese's compliance with the new norms.

Msgr. Charles Scicluna clarified another of the problems in dealing with this issue earlier, in his interview with the Italian newspaper *L'Avvenire*. He explained that between 1975 and 1985, no cases involving pedophile priests were sent to the Congregation for the Doctrine of the Faith, due mainly to some confusion over the interpretation of *graviora delicta* after the promulgation of the 1983 *Code of Canon Law*. With the involvement of Cardinal Ratzinger, Pope John Paul issued several key documents in 2001 that placed the Church's dealings with the crime of pedophilia by priests exclusively under the Congregation. So, as the documentation reveals, by 2001, officials in Rome were aware of the problems that existed in the United States and the need for better oversight in dealing with priests under investigation for sexual abuse. The concern was twofold: to make certain that those acts deemed *graviora delicta* (or very serious crimes) were being handled properly, and to ensure that due process was being followed for both the victims of the sins and crimes and for the accused.

The renewal and reform of the Church's response to clergy sex abuse in Europe follows the same pattern as that embraced in the United States since 2002. Credit goes to many American bishops in leading the effort, but direction comes from Benedict. This has been noted even in the secular press. In a column appearing in the British newspaper *Daily Telegraph*, writer Cristina Odone asserted:

> This Pope has done more than any other churchman to address the issue of priestly child abuse. He has stopped the practice of turning over priests accused of abuse to therapists, as we now know that therapy seldom helps a pedophile. He has fast-tracked the defrocking of priests

found guilty of abuse. He has promoted co-operation, at a diocesan level, between church authorities responsible for canon law and police.

He can point to some real success in the protection of children: in England and Wales, for instance, child protection officers monitor every encounter between children and clergy. The result is that, ironically, there is no safer place for a child today to be than with a Catholic priest.

CHAPTER EIGHT

"I Share in Their Suffering"

I am deeply sorry for the pain and suffering the victims have endured, and I assure them that, as their Pastor, I too share in their suffering.

— Pope Benedict XVI, Homily in Sydney,
Australia, July 19, 2008

With the death of Pope John Paul II and the election of Cardinal Ratzinger as Pope Benedict XVI in April 2005, the Vatican took several high-profile steps to address sexual abuse allegations in a variety of situations.

Pope Benedict was familiar with Archbishop William Levada of San Francisco, who had served in the CDF from 1976 to 1982 and with whom he had worked on the development of the *Catechism of the Catholic Church.* One of the new pope's first decisions was to appoint Archbishop Levada as his successor as head of the Congregation for the Doctrine of the Faith. The appointment was widely seen as the first major statement as to the direction of the new pontificate, and the timing of this historic selection was no accident. Levada — the first American to ever head the powerful office — had extensive experience with abuse cases and, as an American, was familiar with the situation in the United States and the steps taken there to address the crisis.

In the first months after the election of Ratzinger as pope, two lingering cases involving abuse were quickly resolved.

The first case involved Fr. Gino Burresi, a charismatic Italian priest and founder of the Servants of the Immaculate Heart of Mary, seen by some as a latter-day Padre Pio (a sainted mystic and miracle worker in southern Italy). But there were allegations of improper behavior on his part, and in May 2005, Fr. Burresi was barred from public ministry.

More explosive, however, was the second case.

It involved Fr. Marcial Maciel Degollado, the famed founder of the powerful religious order known as the Legionaries of Christ. The Legion, with more than 600 priests, an imposing seminary in Rome, and a large lay movement known as Regnum Christi, was perceived to be one of the popular new religious orders embraced by Pope John Paul II. However, former members had made persistent charges of sexually abusive acts by Fr. Maciel since the 1980s; starting in 2001, the Congregation for the Doctrine of the Faith began an investigation of these allegations.

No decision was rendered for the next four years, and some felt that Fr. Maciel's powerful friendships in the Vatican, including his close relationship with Pope John Paul, had protected him from punishment. This speculation was rendered moot on May 19, 2006, however, when Vatican spokesman Joaquin Navarro-Valls said the Vatican had investigated the claims made by former Legionary seminarians against Fr. Maciel. The conclusion:

> After having submitted the results of the investigation to attentive study, the Congregation for the Doctrine of the Faith, under the guidance of the new prefect, His Eminence Cardinal William Levada, has decided — taking into account both the advanced age of Rev. Maciel and his delicate health — to forego a canonical process and to call the priest to a life reserved to prayer and penance,

renouncing any public ministry. The Holy Father approved these decisions.

This decision shocked his followers, and defenders of the priest, including members of his religious order, initially tried to downplay the significance of the Vatican's decision. After Fr. Maciel's death in 2008, however, they were even more shocked and dismayed to learn that Fr. Maciel had actually had multiple sexual relationships and had fathered at least one child.

The Vatican appointed a panel of five bishops to make a visitation of the order in 2009. Members of the visitation group included Archbishop Charles Chaput of Denver, who conducted investigations of the Legionaries' centers and institutions in the United States and Canada. Mexican Bishop Ricardo Watty Urquidi covered Mexico and Central America; Italian Bishop Giuseppe Versaldi covered Italy, Israel, South Korea, and the Philippines; Chilean Archbishop Ricardo Ezzati Andrello covered South America; and Spanish Bishop Ricardo Blazquez Perez covered Europe outside of Italy. The report of the visitation panel was submitted to the Vatican this year, and the decision of the Vatican regarding the future of the embattled order was expected to follow.

Then in 2009, Archbishop Edwin O'Brien of Baltimore attracted headlines when he made it known that he had told the current head of the order that he could not recommend that anyone in his archdiocese join either the Legionaries or Regnum Christi. The archbishop cited the lack of financial transparency, the cult-like devotion to the founder, and the possible complicity of the order's leadership in the deceptions of Fr. Maciel.

In March 2010, the order finally released a statement admitting that the founder was guilty of abuse of seminarians and of illicit sexual relationships, and it apologized. It also said that any members of the order who had helped in the deception perpetrated by the founder would be held accountable. That Pope Benedict approved the actions taken against Fr. Maciel — and the subsequent investigation of the order — is undeniable. Pope Benedict's actions in the first years of his pontificate showed a forthright desire to address the sexual abuse crisis. He has continued to address the topic repeatedly and directly in a variety of situations.

The first opportunity came in July 2006, when the Irish bishops made their *ad limina* visit (a visit required of all bishops on a rotating five-year schedule) to the Vatican. The meeting followed reports and governmental investigations of widespread sexual abuse of Irish children, and the Church in Ireland was in a state of near-paralysis as the scope of the problem became known.

In the midst of this crisis, the pope addressed the issue in his talk:

> In the exercise of your pastoral ministry, you have had to respond in recent years to many heart-rending cases of sexual abuse of minors. These are all the more tragic when the abuser is a cleric. The wounds caused by such acts run deep, and it is an urgent task to rebuild confidence and trust where these have been damaged. In your continuing efforts to deal effectively with this problem, it is important to establish the truth of what happened in the past, to take whatever steps are necessary to prevent it from occurring again, to ensure that the principles of justice are fully respected and, above all, to bring healing to the victims and to all those affected by these egregious crimes.

That these acts are "crimes," that the truth must be ascertained, and that steps must be taken to prevent further cases were clear priorities for the pope, as was the care of the victims and their families. But the pope also made it clear to the bishops that the path of renewal must pass through this time of repentance:

> In this way, the Church in Ireland will grow stronger and be ever more capable of giving witness to the redemptive power of the Cross of Christ. I pray that by the grace of the Holy Spirit, this time of purification will enable all God's people in Ireland to "maintain and perfect in their lives that holiness which they have received from God."

In 2008, Pope Benedict paid his first visit to the United States. In advance of the trip, there was a great deal of speculation in the media about what, if anything, he would say regarding the sex abuse crisis. The speculation ended on the flight from Rome to Washington, D.C., April 16, when the pope made a point of meeting with journalists and addressing the issue head-on.

The first journalist to ask him a question was John Allen; the question concerned what message the pope was bringing to Catholics who had been suffering from the sexual abuse scandals.

The pope replied in English, as if to make sure that the message would be heard and understood widely.

> It is a great suffering for the Church in the United States and for the Church in general, for me personally, that this could happen. If I read the history of these events, it is difficult for me to understand how it was possible for priests to fail in this way in the mission to give healing, to give God's love to these children. I am ashamed and we will do everything possible to ensure that this does not happen in [the] future.
>
> I think we have to act on three levels: the first is at the level of justice and the political level. I will not speak at

this moment about homosexuality; this is another thing. We will absolutely exclude pedophiles from the sacred ministry; it is absolutely incompatible, and whoever is really guilty of being a pedophile cannot be a priest. So at this first level we can do justice and help the victims, because they are deeply affected; these are the two sides of justice: one, that pedophiles cannot be priests and the other, to help in any possible way the victims.

Then there is the pastoral level. The victims will need healing and help and assistance and reconciliation: This is a big pastoral engagement and I know that the bishops and the priests and all Catholic people in the United States will do whatever possible to help, to assist, to heal.

We have made a visitation of the seminaries and we will do all that is possible in the education of seminarians for a deep spiritual, human and intellectual formation for the students. Only sound persons can be admitted to the priesthood and only persons with a deep personal life in Christ and who have a deep sacramental life. So I know that the bishops and directors of seminarians will do all possible to have a strong, strong discernment because it is more important to have good priests than to have many priests. This is also our third level, and we hope that we can do, and have done and will do in the future, all that is possible to heal these wounds.

Reaction to the pope's comments dominated the next morning's headlines — and, in fact, the events of the next few days worked together to keep the abuse angle regarding the papal visit on the front pages.

The next day, April 16, the pope spoke with the U.S. bishops at the National Shrine of the Immaculate Conception, a speech that addressed a variety of topics — America's Catholic history, the Church's countercultural teachings on many of the hot topics of the day, the role of faith in society, and moral relativism and its impact on American society, including Catholics.

After addressing threats to family life and Catholic marriage, the pope turned to the sexual abuse crisis again:

> Among the countersigns to the Gospel of life found in America and elsewhere is one that causes deep shame: the sexual abuse of minors. Many of you have spoken to me of the enormous pain that your communities have suffered when clerics have betrayed their priestly obligations and duties by such gravely immoral behavior.

The pope praised their efforts to "promote reconciliation and to reach out with loving concern to those so seriously wronged." But he also acknowledged, echoing the words of Cardinal Francis George, that the abuse situation was "sometimes very badly handled":

> Now that the scale and gravity of the problem is more clearly understood, you have been able to adopt more focused remedial and disciplinary measures and to promote a safe environment that gives greater protection to young people.

Next, he sought to place the scandal within a wider context:

> Children deserve to grow up with a healthy understanding of sexuality and its proper place in human relationships. . . . What does it mean to speak of child protection when pornography and violence can be viewed in so many homes through media widely available today? We need to reassess urgently the values underpinning society, so that a sound moral formation can be offered to young people and adults alike.

Finally, he emphasized that the duty of a sound moral formation falls on families, teachers, the media, and particularly the bishops:

> It falls to you, as pastors modeled upon Christ, the Good Shepherd, to proclaim this message loud and clear, and thus to address the sin of abuse within the wider context of sexual *mores*. Moreover, by acknowledging and confronting the problem when it occurs in an ecclesial setting, you can give a lead to others, since this scourge is found not only within your dioceses, but in every sector of society. It calls for a determined, collective response.

Turning next to the bishops' responsibility for their priests, the pope talked frankly about the impact on them of the sordid revelations of abuse by their fellow priests.

> They have experienced shame over what has occurred, and there are those who feel they have lost some of the trust and esteem they once enjoyed. Not a few are experiencing a closeness to Christ in his Passion as they struggle to come to terms with the consequences of the crisis.
> A vital part of your task . . . is to strengthen relationships with your clergy, especially in those cases where tension has arisen between priests and their bishops in the wake of the crisis.

Quoting Pope John Paul II's own words to the U.S. cardinals, Pope Benedict expressed the hope that "this time of trial will bring a purification of the entire Catholic community," leading to "a holier priesthood, a holier episcopate and a holier Church." Such a renewal, he made clear, must start with the bishops:

> If you yourselves live in a manner closely configured to Christ, the Good Shepherd, who laid down his life for his sheep, you will inspire your brother priests to

rededicate themselves to the service of their flocks with Christ-like generosity.

He urged the bishops to spend time in front of the Blessed Sacrament, reciting the Rosary, and praying the Liturgy of the Hours.

The next day, in a homily at Washington Nationals Stadium, the pope spoke to a large audience of lay Catholics as well as priests and bishops, once again turning to the theme of the sexual abuse crisis:

> I acknowledge the pain which the Church in America has experienced as a result of the sexual abuse of minors. No words of mine could describe the pain and harm inflicted by such abuse. It is important that those who have suffered be given loving pastoral attention.
>
> Nor can I adequately describe the damage that has occurred within the community of the Church. Great efforts have already been made to deal honestly and fairly with this tragic situation, and to ensure that children . . . can grow up in a safe environment. These efforts to protect children must continue.

He asked for efforts to heal, help, and reconcile with those who have been hurt, and to pray for their priests.

That same day, the pope had a private meeting with five victims of the clerical sex abusers in the Boston archdiocese. While the meeting was closed to the press, it was deemed a watershed moment, and the victims at that time spoke warmly of the encounter with the pontiff.

(Two years later, in his pastoral letter to the Irish Catholic Church, Pope Benedict wrote, "On several occasions since my election to the See of Peter, I have met with victims of sexual abuse, as indeed I am ready to do in the future. I have sat with them, I have listened to their stories, I have acknowledged their suffering, and I have prayed with them and for them." Such meetings have generally been off the record and behind the scenes, and not used as some sort of journalism-driven spectacle.) At the end of the visit — although some U.S. Catholic observers grumbled that the pope had taken his own visit off track by addressing the issue so directly — the overall impact was strongly positive. The pope was making it clear that he understood the scope of the problem and its significance for the U.S. Church, and showed his determination to address the issue head-on.

His next opportunity arose just months later, when he traveled to Australia in July for World Youth Day. Australia had also been plagued by a long-running sex abuse scandal, with an estimated 1,000 victims. Again, the pope addressed the issue on his flight to the country, reiterating the same points he had made while flying to the United States and focusing on the moral challenge of the abuse crisis and the role that priests should play.

In looking at the training of priests, he asked:

> . . . what was insufficient in our education, in our teaching in recent decades: there was, in the 50s, 60s and 70s, the idea of proportionalism in ethics: It held that nothing is bad in itself, but only in proportion to others; with proportionalism it was possible to think for some subjects — one could also be pedophilia — that in some proportion they could be a good thing. Now, it must be stated clearly, this was never Catholic doctrine. There are things which are always bad, and pedophilia is always bad. In our education, in the seminaries, in our permanent formation of the priests, we have to help priests to really be close to Christ, to learn from Christ, and so to be helpers, and not adversaries of our fellow human beings, of our Christians.

In a July 19 Mass, the pope apologized for clergy sexual abuse.

In his homily, Pope Benedict said he wanted "to pause to acknowledge the shame which we have all felt as a result of the sexual abuse of minors by some clergy and religious in this country."

Catholic News Service reported that, in an addition to his prepared text, he said:

> I am deeply sorry for the pain and suffering the victims have endured, and I assure them that as their pastor, I, too, share in their suffering.
>
> These misdeeds, which constitute so grave a betrayal of trust, deserve unequivocal condemnation. They have caused great pain and have damaged the Church's witness.

The pope encouraged the implementation of programs to protect children and screen out abusers, saying that such reforms were necessary "in combating this evil." And again, he reiterated:

> Victims should receive compassion and care, and those responsible for these evils must be brought to justice.

As he did during his visit to the United States, the pontiff met with Australian victims. It was a private meeting out of respect for the victims, but the press was informed. He has also met with victims at the Vatican (members of First Nations from Canada) in April 2009, as well as with other victims in Malta in 2010, and has stated that he is ready to meet victims again, especially those from Ireland.

While Pope Benedict had made known his willingness to confront the issue of sexual abuse, this in no way stopped the eruption of sexual abuse cases in various parts of the Catholic world. As has been documented in earlier chapters, perhaps the worst affected was Ireland, in part because it had for so long been a bulwark of the Catholic faith.

One of the heads of the Irish Church, and a key figure both in preparing the Irish people for the impact of the Ryan and Murphy reports and accepting the report's harsh conclusions regarding the Church's bishops, was Archbishop Diarmuid Martin of Dublin. Archbishop Martin, a longtime Vatican official, had served in the Vatican councils for the family and for justice and peace and represented the Vatican in Geneva prior to his Dublin appointment. In the shattering aftermath of the reports, the Holy Father called a summit of twenty-four Irish bishops, who met with the pontiff and ten top Vatican officials on February 15 and 16, 2010. The meeting provided a forum for the bishops to meet with the pope and explain their own actions as well as suggest ways to promote healing.

A private meeting was also held between the Holy Father and Bishop Denis Brennan, the bishop of Ferns since March 2006, who had inherited a disastrous situation in the diocese. According to the Ferns Report, a study of the sex abuse problem in the diocese from 1962 to 2002, there were some 100 cases. These led to civil suits that resulted in the diocese owing millions of Euros in damages, with more to come in the next years. The pope used the session as an opportunity to become even more personally familiar with the problems in Ireland and expressed his horror at the details.

Out of the meeting came a communiqué from the Vatican that included the following:

> For his part, the Holy Father observed that the sexual abuse of children and young people is not only a heinous crime, but also a grave sin which offends God and wounds the dignity of the human person created in his image. While realizing that the current painful situation will not be resolved quickly, he challenged the Bishops

to address the problems of the past with determination and resolve, and to face the present crisis with honesty and courage. He also expressed the hope that the present meeting would help to unify the Bishops and enable them to speak with one voice in identifying concrete steps aimed at bringing healing to those who had been abused, encouraging a renewal of faith in Christ and restoring the Church's spiritual and moral credibility.

It also acknowledged "errors of judgment and omissions" by Church leaders:

> All those present recognized that this grave crisis has led to a breakdown in trust in the Church's leadership and had damaged her witness to the Gospel and its moral teaching.

The pope promised a letter to the Irish people that would say more. But the final statement, released at the end of the meeting, was poorly received by the Irish press because of its lack of specificity regarding next steps — a lack largely due to the fact that the bishops had already established policies and procedures to safeguard children, including cooperating with civil authorities. And, while the statement expressed the hope that the Irish bishops would speak with one voice, the conference itself has been divided; four bishops have offered to resign, and rumors have circulated that past and present church leaders were resentful of Archbishop Martin's forthright condemnation of previous actions.

However, only weeks later, the promised "Pastoral Letter of the Holy Father Pope Benedict XVI to the Catholics of Ireland" was released on the Feast of St. Joseph, March 19, and read or distributed in Irish parishes on March 21.

This letter, striking in its clarity of expression and the directness of its statements, was the pope's most significant and most powerful reflection on the clergy abuse crisis, weaving together themes already addressed, but with a heartfelt emphasis.

It began with the pope declaring:

> I can only share in the dismay and the sense of betrayal that so many of you have experienced on learning of these sinful and criminal acts and the way Church authorities in Ireland dealt with them.
>
> For my part, considering the gravity of these offenses, and the often inadequate response to them on the part of the ecclesiastical authorities in your country, I have decided to write this Pastoral Letter to express my closeness to you and to propose a path of healing, renewal and reparation.

First and foremost, the pope asked for an honest admission of fault:

> In order to recover from this grievous wound, the Church in Ireland must first acknowledge before the Lord and before others the serious sins committed against defenseless children.

And to the victims and their families, the pope's apology for crimes committed against them was direct and without equivocation.

> You have suffered grievously, and I am truly sorry. I know that nothing can undo the wrong you have endured. Your trust has been betrayed and your dignity has been violated. Many of you found that, when you were courageous enough to speak of what happened to you, no one would listen. Those of you who were abused in residential institutions must have felt that there was no escape from your sufferings.

He also acknowledged, "It is understandable that you find it hard to forgive or be reconciled with the Church. In her name, I openly express the shame and remorse that we all feel."

His tone to the priest abusers, and to the bishops who did not address their crimes, was much tougher. To abusers, he wrote:

> You betrayed the trust that was placed in you by innocent young people and their parents, and you must answer for it before Almighty God and before properly constituted tribunals.
>
> Together with the immense harm done to victims, great damage has been done to the Church and to the public perception of the priesthood and religious life.

While he did remind them of the ultimate mercy of God, he made it clear that they must openly acknowledge their guilt and submit to the demands of justice.

With regard to the bishops, he was equally blunt:

> Some of you and your predecessors failed, at times grievously, to apply the long-established norms of canon law to the crime of child abuse.

The pope referred to "grave errors of judgment" and "failure of leadership." He told them to fully implement the norms of canon law and to cooperate with civil authorities "in their area of competence":

> Only decisive action carried out with complete honesty and transparency will restore the respect and good will of the Irish people towards the Church to which we have consecrated our lives.

Echoing points he made when talking to the U.S. bishops in Washington two years before, he urged the bishops to renew themselves and their own spiritual lives so as to be proper examples to their priests and to help in the formation of the Irish lay faithful.

The Irish people rightly expect you to be men of God, to be holy, to live simply, to pursue personal conversion daily. For them, in the words of St. Augustine, you are a bishop; yet with them you are called to be a follower of Christ.

The pope also addressed comments to parents, to Irish young people, and to the vast majority of priests and religious who did nothing wrong, yet now must carry this burden:

Many of you feel personally discouraged, even abandoned. I am also aware that in some people's eyes you are tainted by association and viewed as if you were somehow responsible for the misdeeds of others.

He also acknowledged that many priests are "disappointed, bewildered, and angered by the way these matters have been handled by some of your superiors."

In the letter, Pope Benedict suggests some of the causes of the crisis — poor screening of candidates for the priesthood, "insufficient human, moral, intellectual, and spiritual formation" of seminarians, "a tendency in society to favor the clergy and other authority figures," and "a misplaced concern for the reputation of the Church and the avoidance of scandal."

He also took note of the decline in traditional Catholic devotional practices, and expressed concern that, after Vatican II, "there was a well-intentioned but misguided tendency to avoid penal approaches to canonically irregular situations."

Pope Benedict concludes his letter to Irish Catholics with specific suggestions to address the situation. While he has already affirmed the criminal nature of the abuse and the canonical and civil actions that are called for, in the pope's mind — and as expressed in almost all of his other references to the scandals — the crisis is ultimately spiritual.

It should be no surprise, therefore, that his "concrete initiatives to address the situation" are spiritual as well. He offered up six initiatives for Irish Catholics:

1. To devote all Friday penances for a period of one year "to pray for an outpouring of God's mercy and the Holy Spirit's gifts of holiness and strength upon the Church in your country."

2. To offer up "your fasting, your prayer, your reading of Scripture, and your works of mercy in order to obtain the grace of healing and renewal for the Church in Ireland."

3. "To discover anew the sacrament of Reconciliation."

4. To pay attention to Eucharistic Adoration. The pope asked that every diocese have churches and chapels devoted to this practice, and he particularly asked seminaries, religious houses, and monasteries to devote time to this practice.

5. To cooperate with an "apostolic visitation" of certain dioceses, seminaries, and religious congregations, which would involve both the local Church and offices of the Roman curia.

6. Finally, he asked for a "nationwide Mission to be held for all bishops, priests, and religious."

In a press conference after Mass on March 20, Archbishop Martin again made headlines of with his call to his fellow bishops to take responsibility for the Irish Church's failures. "Without accountability for the past," Archbishop Martin told reporters outside his cathedral in Dublin, "there will be no healing and no trust for the future."

According to Catholic News Service, Archbishop Martin described the letter as "part of a strategy of a renewal of the

Church." Asked why the pope did not make any reference to a Vatican role in the crisis in Ireland, Archbishop Martin said, the responsibility "very much" fell on the Irish church. "The Vatican had produced the norms of canon law and they weren't respected in the management of these cases," he said.

In the months ahead, more cases are likely to attract public attention and keep the news of the clergy sexual abuse crisis on the front pages of many newspapers. At one time, the crisis was viewed as primarily an American problem; today, however, reports of abuse allegations surface not only from throughout Europe but also in Latin America and Asia.

Sexual abuse is a worldwide problem, so it should not be surprising that it is a problem that confronts the Church as well. What remains devastating are the allegations and the evidence that leaders of the Church responded inadequately to reports of abuse, worried more about the potential impact on the Church of any scandal, or put undue reliance on the advice of others regarding the rehabilitation of abusive priests.

For Archbishop — later Cardinal — Ratzinger, appreciation of the gravity of the abuse crisis and its long-term implications of the Church grew slowly over time. From 2001 on, because of his role as head of the doctrinal congregation, he had perhaps the broadest perspective on the worldwide dimensions of the crisis of anyone in the Church, and the most detailed knowledge of the heinous nature of the crimes. Thanks to the 2001 reform of the procedures for handling abuse cases at the Vatican, the Congregation then and now has been able to speed resolution of cases — a change in process that clearly reflected Cardinal Ratzinger's understanding of the urgency of the crisis.

As pope, he has attempted to address the crisis in a variety of forums: meeting with victims, challenging bishops, and resolving some of the highest profile allegations. But the cases keep coming, and with a variety of legal actions underway seeking to fix responsibility for the crisis on the Vatican or even the pope himself, it is likely that the rest of Pope Benedict's pontificate will be consumed by the scandal.

Pope Benedict, of all people, knows that this may simply be the price that must be paid.

In his interview with Peter Seewald in the book *Salt of the Earth*, then-Cardinal Ratzinger spoke of his years in Munich and the conflicts into which he was drawn as he sought to challenge some of the prevailing trends in the Church.

> The words of the Bible and the Church Fathers rang in my ears, those sharp condemnations of shepherds who are like mute dogs; in order to avoid conflicts, they let the poison spread. Peace is not the first civic duty, and a bishop whose only concern is not to have any problems and to gloss over as many conflicts as possible is an image I find repulsive.

For Pope Benedict, no price will be too high if the poison's spread is halted.

Conclusion

*In confronting the present crisis, measures to deal justly
with individual crimes are essential, yet on their own
they are not enough: a new vision is needed, to inspire
present and future generations to treasure the gift of our
common faith.*

— Pope Benedict XVI, Pastoral Letter to the
Catholics of Ireland

The clergy sexual abuse crisis — the name given to three
decades of scandalous revelations regarding the actions of some
priests and the actions or inaction of some bishops — will most
likely define the pontificate of Pope Benedict XVI.

This is not so much because of the recent flurry of allegations regarding the pope himself — which are, in the words of
one Vatican lawyer, a "rush to judgment" at best. Rather, it is
because Pope Benedict, both as head of the Congregation for
the Doctrine of the Faith and as pope, has played a historically
pivotal role in the Vatican's response to the crisis: From leading
the CDF's efforts before and after 2001 in reviewing the case
files of suspect priests to his own efforts to address the issue
forthrightly as pope, Benedict has grown into a leadership role
on this issue just when the Church has most needed him. He
has met with victims. He has rebuked the abuser priests. He
has challenged the bishops. He has overseen a series of proce-
dural reforms that have allowed the Church to respond more
quickly when it is necessary to restrict, suspend, or even laicize
a priest.

As Cardinal Sean O'Malley of Boston commented on calls for the pope's resignation:

> There is much confusion and misinformation about the Holy Father's historic role in dealing with the problem of sexual abuse of children by clergy. What is very clear to me — and I think to all who are fair-minded — is that Cardinal Ratzinger and later Pope Benedict has been dedicated to eradicating sexual abuse in the Church and trying to rectify the mistakes of the past. Until the sexual abuse crisis really became part of the consciousness of the Church in Europe, there were many who were unsympathetic to our efforts in the U.S. to deal with the problem in a transparent way and assure that our Catholic schools, parishes and agencies would be safe for children.
>
> During this period of at least a decade, the strongest ally we had in this effort was Cardinal Ratzinger. As head of the Congregation for the Doctrine of the Faith, he allowed us to move forward with the Essential Norms which became local Church law in the U.S. and facilitated the *Charter for the Protection of Children and Young People.*

It is clear that Benedict has a high and demanding theology regarding the roles of priest and bishop, believing that they should live exemplary lives and be models of Christlike behavior for their colleagues and their people. Like many of his generation, he may have been slow to imagine the acts of depravity by some who were ordained for the service of God, and the numbers of those who violated their priestly vows and the trust of children, of youth, of seminarians, and of their families.

What is striking is that Ratzinger *did* change. If at one point he had mirrored the naïveté or the misunderstandings of many of his generation, he has evolved into a historic advocate for the reform and the renewal of the Church, and he understands the significance of the struggle.

There are, in fact, four significant steps he has taken as pope.

First, he appointed Archbishop Levada as head, or prefect, of the Congregation for the Doctrine of the Faith. He chose an American who was aware of the scale and scope of the scandals and had no need to "get up to speed" on the issue.

Second, he was willing to address the situation directly. He made it clear by his example that keeping silent to "avoid scandal" was not an option for a Church leader. Taking action against the founder of the Legionaries of Christ was particularly noteworthy, for he was not deterred by power, influence, or the shock that such a move would cause.

Third, he was willing to speak in plain language to all of the parties, as evidenced in his letter to Irish Catholics — a remarkable papal document that apologizes, rebukes, and chides with admirable directness.

Fourth, he understood that, at its heart, this crisis is first and foremost a spiritual challenge to the entire Church.

Benedict knows from Church history, going back to the Acts of the Apostles, that God has often been betrayed by his creatures in whom He puts much trust. In an interview with Peter Seewald in *God and the World*, he addressed the question of why there are bad priests and bad bishops:

> The strange thing is that God entrusts himself to such fragile vessels. That he has taken such a horrible risk with the Church. He has put himself into hands that betray him time and again. And he has often left us the opportunity of falling and of being corrupted, so that he still has to support the Church himself again and again through these very tools that have proved unsuitable.

Benedict understands that the spiritual challenge must be addressed on multiple fronts.

There is the pastoral challenge itself. Children have been wronged by those who represented the Church. Christ himself addresses the drama of such betrayal, when he says:

> "Whoever causes one of these little ones who believe in me to sin, it would be better for him if a great millstone were hung round his neck and he were thrown into the sea."
>
> — Mk 9:42

Pope Benedict has made it clear that he understands the depth of the betrayal, acknowledging that even when victims found the courage to speak up, "no one would listen" (Irish letter). He has met and spoken with the victims in private. He has read the files. He understands the depth of the "filth."

At the same time, he knows that the hardest spiritual truth is that healing comes from forgiveness and reconciliation. Even as he identifies with the victims' profound sense of betrayal, he respectfully calls on them to see in Christ's own wounds "the very means by which the power of evil is broken and we are reborn to life and hope." He begs the victims and their family to draw nearer to Christ as a means to finding "reconciliation, deep inner healing, and peace." And finally, he admits the need for "a Church purified by penance and renewed in pastoral charity."

During a homily on April 15, 2010, at Mass with members of the Pontifical Biblical Commission, he elaborated:

> I must say that we Christians, even in recent times, have often avoided the word "penance," which seemed too harsh to us. Now, under the attacks of the world that speaks to us of our sins, we see that being able to do penance is a grace. We see how it is necessary to do penance, that is, to recognize what is mistaken in our life.

Benedict is pleading for a spiritual renewal that must encompass the entire Church, from bishop to priest to lay person. If we understand ourselves as one people, one body in Christ, then there will be no real solution that does not involve the entire people. We must all rededicate ourseleves to prayer, fasting, and repentance for the reform and the renewal of the Church.

This is a difficult lesson, the pope understands. From the beginning, the sense of betrayal on the part of ordinary Catholics has led many to conclude that this was not primarily a problem of priests doing wrong but of bishops failing in their duties to oversee those priests and protect the faithful. Most of the faithful do not see this as "their spiritual problem" but a problem of the Church's leadership.

The pope has not been reluctant to challenge the bishops, calling them to a life of greater spiritual renewal. He has also been willing to accept the resignations of bishops who have been actively involved in covering up instances of clergy sexual abuse, at least as seen in the Irish scandal. There are, understandably, critics who argue that this is not enough. The fact is, however, that more than 60 percent of the bishops who were in Dallas in 2002 have retired or moved on, and a new wave of leaders has taken their place.

But such renewal, to be truly effective, must involve the entire Church. In the Pastoral Letter to the Catholics of Ireland, as in many other statements and speeches, he repeatedly asks that Catholics sacrifice and pray for an outpouring of graces upon the Church. The reform and the renewal of the Church must start with each one of us. The impact of the scandals on the faith lives of the ordinary Catholic is hard to quantify, but one certainly hears anecdotal evidence from Catholics that the current round of scandals has "shaken their faith in the Church"; a few say they may leave it. While one is sympathetic to the sense of betrayal, one is also tempted to ask if they know nothing of

Church history. If, in the words of Pope St. Gregory the Great, the "Church is always renewing itself," it is because it is always in need of renewal. We are a Church of sinners, and the history of the Church is of God's great revelation entrusted to the "weak vessels." Catholics have committed sins of commission and omission throughout the Church's history. Thankfully, the history of the Church also shows us that great men and women rise up to help purify and renew it when this is most needed.

While admitting that the Church is in need of renewal and reform today, it must also be addressed forthrightly that the Church itself has been singled out for extraordinary attention and condemnation, and that there are many agendas at work in the current round of controversies.

It is equally undeniable that the exposure of children to abuse is intolerable, and that the media has performed a service in forcing the Church's leaders to examine their own actions and repent of their sins. That victims and their families deserve our thanks for speaking out, and deserve just compensation to help repair the damage done to them, is equally undeniable.

Nevertheless, Catholics must also strongly reject the impression being given by some of the media coverage that the Church is somehow unusual in the number of incidents of abusers, or that this is just a "Catholic problem." Indeed, what is worrisome about the recurring waves of media coverage is that many are beginning to define the Church as permanently tainted by this crime.

No other organization has studied its own history with the problem so thoroughly as the Church in the United States; in doing so, it has found rates of abuse similar to those estimated in general society. Indeed, statistics suggest that most children have a much greater risk of being abused in their families or in their schools than by a Catholic priest. This is certainly no reason for Catholics to celebrate or to cease to be vigilant — but at the same time, the stigma the Church now wears is one that should indict our entire society.

And if priestly celibacy is the problem, as some routinely suggest, then there should not be such widespread incidents of child sexual abuse in the general population or in families. But, of course, there are.

Statistics vary, but the government estimates that one out of every twelve public school students will likely suffer some sexually abusive experience before he or she graduates from high school. Yet, because most public schools are sheltered from being sued for punitive damages, there is not nearly the focused legal attention that is being placed on the Catholic Church.

Which brings us to a second necessary point: many people are exploiting the current situation. First, there are the lawyers. Recent allegations involving Pope Benedict have come from documents provided by a lawyer who is going to the U.S. Supreme Court to draw the Vatican in as a defendant in his civil suits.

The Church in the United States alone has spent already upwards of $2 billion settling abuse claims and providing assistance to both the victims and the perpetrators of abuse. No other organization in the world comes close to spending this amount on this issue — with about $700 million going to lawyers. The impact has been significant on nearly every diocese, impacting the funding of many socially worthwhile projects — and, in fact, leading to the actual bankruptcy of seven dioceses so far.

But others who seek to profit from the travails of the Church include many Catholics with their own ideological axes to grind: lobbyists for every possible agenda from women priests, an end of celibacy, or calls for a Third Vatican Council, to rejections of the changes mandated by Vatican II. Whenever there is a new wave of attention given to sexual abuse cases, eager attention is given to the various agendas of the Church's internal critics.

Most recently, commentators and critics have argued that Pope Benedict should resign from the papacy. Not only would such an act be virtually without precedent; it flies in the face of the leadership that Benedict has been providing on this issue.

The critics of the Church have had a field day bringing a host of charges against the Vatican, against the pope, and against the Church. The media involved, unfortunately, have given far less attention to determining the validity of any accusations than simply reporting them breathlessly. Because so many of the details of the individual cases are so horrific, such as the Murphy case in Milwaukee, the details regarding the Vatican's involvement are often obscured and the conclusions rushed.

The Vatican has also at times been less than effective in getting its response out in an effective and timely fashion. It has been disturbing for many Catholics, after all of our many years of experience dealing with revelations of scandal, that in 2010 we seem to be no better as a Church with dealing openly, forthrightly, and transparently with these issues than we were in 1985. Many Catholics are desperate to hear the Church's side of the story, but too many pulpits are silent, and too many leaders have fumbled the opportunities to speak out with charity and clarity.

Yet all of this is, in many ways, the price that must be paid for not having addressed the intolerable for so long. Whatever we Catholics may think of the motivations of our critics, we must first and foremost be dedicated to the exposure of the truth. Only when the truth is revealed can we know how we must reform ourselves and our Church to act more justly in the future.

Cardinal Ratzinger said as much in his 1997 interview with Peter Seewald in *Salt of the Earth,* when he answered a question about acknowledging the Church's past errors.

I think that truthfulness is always an essential virtue, especially so that we better realize what the Church is and isn't. In this sense, a new, sober look, if one wants to put it like that, which doesn't conceal the shadowy sides of the Church's history, is very important for the sake of honesty and truthfulness. And if, as it were, confession, assessment, recognition, acknowledgement of one's own guilt is an essential part of being Christian, because only by admitting the truths about myself can I learn to act rightly . . .

Confession. Assessment. Recognition. Acknowledgement of one's own guilt. In many ways, this has been the agenda of the U.S., English, Australian, and now Irish churches. And now, it must be the agenda of the Universal Church as well.

In the spirit of reform and renewal, there are three courses of action that the Church Universal might embrace as it moves forward and seeks to put these scandals behind it:

First, the clear tone of accountability that the pope has already established must be continued. Perpetrators who have abused children must be held accountable both in the civil judicial systems (if there is enough material evidence for a trial) and in the Church administrative and canonical review. This accountability must extend, where applicable, to the bishops themselves; the Church must be as honest as the pope was in his letter to Irish Catholics in holding the bishops accountable. Much of the anger among the Catholic laity, and much of the suffering among the thousands of good and faithful Catholic priests, is caused by the impression that their own bishops had let them down, while suffering little in the way of consequences.

Accountability should also extend to the Vatican. The pope has shown that he is willing to apologize, and it would be a step forward for the Vatican to admit that its officials and departments were slow to see the scale of the crisis and to respond adequately, even as the Holy See has made major strides to address this shortcoming.

Second, and related to this, the Church must look at the policies it implements worldwide and at the Vatican. The Vatican has made clear what was long implicit — that civil authorities must be informed of abuse allegations. It would be a benefit for the whole Church if the pope were now to make the norms implemented in the United States and England the policy for the rest of the Church. The rights of the accused as well as the rights of the victims must be honored, and to the extent that it is possible, there should be consistency in the implementation of these norms throughout the Church. But justice must be done. Whether "zero tolerance" should be the norm in all cases is the subject of ongoing debate, for the Church must act with mercy as well as justice. But never should the abuse of minors by someone in authority or representing the Church be tolerated.

Likewise, the Church should become an example for all governments and organizations in its efforts to protect children. While there has been and will continue to be debates and discussions about how best to do this, what cannot be denied is that the Church in the United States has implemented an extraordinarily thorough review of its priests and religious, its seminary candidates, its lay employees, and its volunteers. As George Weigel wrote in an essay for *First Things*, "The Catholic Church is, by empirical measure, the safest environment for young people in America today."

Third, the renewal of the priesthood and the religious life must continue, with the ultimate aim of renewing the entire People of God in their relationship with Christ. This means more than just tightening the review process for seminary candidates. The formation of seminarians must be improved as well, and studies such as the recent visitation of U.S. seminaries must be encouraged worldwide.

More importantly, the spiritual renewal of the religious life means that a greater emphasis must be placed on the relationship of the priest with the Lord. This relationship must be dynamic and vital so that the priest can live his vocation to the fullest and be a true witness to his faith.

No charter, program, or papal speech will root out all traces of sin. Church history tells us that sin is ever present, and that renewal is always needed. But, as Dublin Archbishop Diarmuid Martin put it in his March 20, 2010, homily:

> Our prayer this evening is that this period of renewal in the Church will be a moment of healing. A precondition of healing is recognition and rejection of the faults of the past, without becoming entrenched and immobilized in history.
>
> The truth must come out; without the truth we will never be truly free.
>
> We must face the truth of the past; repent it; make good the damage done. And yet we must move forward day by day along the painful path of renewal, knowing that it is only when our human misery encounters face-to-face the liberating mercy of God that our Church will be truly restored and enriched.

Prayer for Pope Benedict XVI

Lord, source of eternal life and truth,
give to your shepherd, Benedict, a spirit
of courage and right judgment, a spirit
of knowledge and love. By governing
with fidelity those entrusted to his care,
may he, as successor to the Apostle
Peter and Vicar of Christ, build your
Church into a sacrament of unity, love,
and peace for all the world. Amen.

V/ Let us pray for Benedict, the pope.
R/ May the Lord preserve him,
give him a long life,
make him blessed upon the earth,
and not hand him over
to the power of his enemies.
V/ May your hand
be upon your holy servant.
R/ And upon your son,
whom you have anointed.

Appendices

The Perspective of Canon Law
by Msgr. William King, J.C.D.

A commentary on the the apostolic letter (*motu proprio*) *Sacramentorum Sanctitatis Tutela*, promulgating the norms on the more serious offenses reserved to the Congregation for the Doctrine of the Faith, April 30, 2001; and the Letter reserving to the Congregation for the Doctrine of the Faith grave offences, May 18, 2001

The Catholic Church is not primarily a community of laws. Our community is based before all else on our relationship with Jesus Christ. In Him, the head of the Church, we are in relationship or communion with the bishops and with one another in the Body of Christ. Law exists within this set of relationships primarily to promote, protect and defend the values that are most important and most essential to the Church, while assisting us toward salvation in Christ. Law exists within the Church to enable Catholics to participate fully in the life of the faith community and to protect their right to do so. Law also serves to protect the Church from the unloving and to ensure the good order of the Body of Christ.

Since the beginning of the Church, questions have arisen about just how to ensure the good order of the Church. The Apostles and others frequently came to Jesus with questions about fasting and conduct. Jesus Himself gave the Church the first norms for how to correct a fellow believer who may have done wrong (Mt 18:15-17). The Acts of the Apostles tells us of a gathering of the Apostles for the express purpose of making a decision about what rules should apply to new Christians (Acts

2:15-29). Gathered with Peter, their head, the Apostles discussed and determined how new converts would be treated, and what minimum expectations would be imposed upon them.

Popes since St. Peter have been faced with questions that affect the community of believers, and popes have enacted laws for the Church in every century.

Law in the Church is called "canon law." The Greek word *kanon* describes a measuring rod, a type of ruler or yardstick. Canon law is a standard of behavior for persons whose goal is to live in a graced relationship with God. Because canon law is for a global Church, the particular canons or laws are often stated in broad terms, sometimes allowing the diocesan bishop to interpret or adapt the general norms as needed in the local environment, employing what is termed the principle of subsidiarity. Because canon law is rooted in our relationship with Christ, the canons are often stated in theological terms or have a basis in theology. This is important to understand, since the foundation and ultimate object of canon law are different from secular state or federal law.

It is surprising to some that the Church has a complete system of law, providing for administrative, legislative, and judicial functions of pastoral governance. Indeed, life within the Church presupposes that charity will animate the mutual relations that comprise the Church, and that mercy will motivate a response to transgressions. However, human nature remains vulnerable to sin, and sins bear consequences for the entire Body of Christ.

Most of the canons do not impose obligations, but instead define roles and responsibilities and the proper way of doing things in a global Church. For instance, the *Code of Canon Law*, currently the principal source of law for the Church, defines what a diocese is, a bishop, a pastor, and lists some of the rights and responsibilities that lay persons and clergy have in the Church. It provides for structures of consultation and imposes certain fiscal controls in dioceses and religious institutes or Orders. It also states what behaviors are unacceptable among the members of the Body of Christ, and goes so far as to identify a few behaviors that are so serious they are considered religious crimes within the Church.

In a 1979 address to the Roman Rota, one of the tribunals of the Holy See, Pope John Paul II summarized the nature of criminal or penal law in the Church:

> In the vision of a Church which protects the rights of each faithful, but which furthermore promotes and protects the common good as an indispensible condition for the integral development of the human and Christian person, a penal discipline also plays a positive role: . . . a means to repair the deficiencies of the individual good and in the common good which were manifest in the anti-ecclesial, offensive, and scandalous behavior of certain members of the people of God.

In fact, canon 1341 of the Church's current law defines three objectives of penal or criminal law in the Church: to repair scandal, restore justice, and reform the offender. It can be said that the notion of crime within the Church recognizes that certain serious, and sinful, acts disrupt the communion of the Church by causing scandal and creating injustice. When many hear the word "scandal" today they think only of the secular meaning — something that was better kept hidden. However, the Church uses the word in a very different way. Deriving from its root in the Greek word *skandalon*, a word that describes an obstacle over which someone might trip or stumble, the Church speaks of *scandal* as an action which may be a stumbling block to deeper faith or to salvation. Scandal in the Church describes an obstacle to the believer following the path of salvation in Christ.

To answer legal questions, such as whether a person committed an ecclesiastical crime, canon law also sets up a court or tribunal system within the Church. The largest section of canons in the *Code of Canon Law* is intended to regulate that judicial system.

It is important to understand that not every violation of canon law is a crime, nor does every violation of canon law have a penalty attached to it. In fact, very few negative behaviors in the Church call for penalties. For the most part, the Church relies on God's Grace working through a properly formed conscience, or the Grace of the Sacrament of Penance, to correct moral failings. However, there are a few behaviors that are so offensive or hurtful that they call for a penalty. Canons 1364 through 1399 list those specific offenses that call for a penalty. A successfully procured abortion is one such act. Desecration of the Holy Eucharist is another. The sexual abuse of a minor by a cleric (deacon, priest, or bishop) is also among those crimes demanding a just penalty.

There are two types of penalties in the Church. Formally they are called *censures* and *expiatory penalties*, but informally censures are often termed "medicinal penalties."

A censure has the purpose of acting like a medicine for the soul, and it is meant to be a temporary measure, prompting an end to the offensive behavior. There are three such penalties: suspension, interdict, and excommunication. Each of these deprives a person of some spiritual good or pastoral function. By depriving him of this, the intent is to reform the conscience and heart of the offender and bring him to repentance and a change of heart. When that occurs, the censure is to be lifted.

An expiatory penalty, on the other hand, is intended not to reform but to punish the offender, so as to repair the scandal, deter the offending behavior in others, and restore justice for the victims and community. In the earlier (1917) *Code of Canon Law*, this type of penalty was called a "vindictive" penalty. It may be a permanent punishment if the serious nature of the offense warrants it, or if the offender remains unrepentant. Two examples of an expiatory penalty are removal from an office within the Church and dismissal from the clerical state — what the secular media often terms "defrocking."

The word "defrocking" may be dramatic in its imagery, but it is not a term of canon law. To understand the Church's approach to the punishment of priests, we should consider what is meant in Catholic theology and law by ordination and priestly ministry.

There are three components to priestly ministry in theology and canon law. The first is the sacrament of Holy Orders itself, by which a man — after a lengthy period of instruction, study, and spiritual formation — is configured to the person of Christ and given capacity by the grace of the sacrament to function as a sacred minister within the community of faithful. This sacrament spiritually impresses a sacred character upon the recipient, which — like the character imposed by the sacraments of Baptism and Confirmation — is indelible and perpetual. Given by God, it cannot be removed by the Church. The second component is the canonical or legal relationship with the community, which arises not by sacramental grace but by operation of canon law. This is called the "clerical state," which is to say the legal status of clergy within the Church. The third component is the empowerment to act as a deacon or priest or bishop, and this is usually expressed in the form of faculties conferred by the law and attached to an office, such as pastor, or faculties granted by a bishop. All three components are required for priestly ministry: Holy Orders alone does not give a priest the authority to exercise ministry in the Church.

These three components are regulated in canon law — the permanent character of the sacrament of Holy Orders, the legal relationship that arises from the clerical state, and the empowerment to act as a sacred minister through the exercise of ministerial faculties. The sacramental reality of Holy Orders is not subject to a penalty, since it is a Grace conferred by Christ Jesus. Once the sacrament has been received, no penalty can erase the indelible character of Holy Orders. Like the sacraments of Baptism and Confirmation, the sacrament of Holy Orders cannot be reversed by imposing a penalty. However, this is not to say that an offending cleric is beyond punishment by the Church. When questions arise as to the appropriate punishment for an offending cleric, a penalty may address either of the other two components — the clerical state, or the faculties needed to exercise ministry — but not Holy Orders itself. It is for this reason that it is sometimes said, "Once a priest, always a priest."

In practice, what does this mean? There are two states of legal personhood within the Church: laity and clergy, or the lay state and the clerical state. When a man receives the sacrament of Holy Orders as a deacon, whether that person remains a permanent deacon or later becomes a priest or bishop, the law determines that he enters the clerical state (prior to Pope Paul VI's revision of ecclesial ministries in 1968, it was with the reception of tonsure and not diaconate that a man entered the clerical state). Possessing the clerical state, he is considered part of the clergy of the Church, that is to say a cleric. Something more is then needed for him to exercise ministry. He needs an additional element: faculties to be legally empowered to function in ministry. Without a faculty granted by a bishop, for example, no priest can validly absolve sins, except in danger of death. Although the sacramental character of Holy Orders, once validly received, is beyond the Church's system of penalties, canon law provides penalties which can affect a cleric's ability to exercise ministry, either by affecting his ministerial faculties or removing his clerical status.

Because different behaviors cause different types of harm, there are degrees of penalties that can be imposed. A priest may be suspended from office (say, that of pastor) for a time, or may be removed permanently from office. A priest may have some of his faculties restricted, so that he may not hear confessions or absolve from sins, or he may have all his priestly faculties suspended, revoked, or limited. The most serious penalties, however, are reserved for the most serious crimes. In certain especially offensive crimes, a cleric may be dismissed from the clerical state, which is always a permanent penalty and is what the secular media calls "defrocking." However, any of these penalties has the same effect in practice. The result is, in effect, akin to withdrawing a physician's license to practice medicine, or disbarring a lawyer. Without faculties a priest may not function, as is also true if he is dismissed from the clerical state.

As in any legal system, even in canon law the mere presence of a law and the threat of a serious penalty do not by themselves guarantee compliance. Individuals may choose to ignore the precepts of a law. This is true of those clerics who did sexually molest children and teenagers, and it is equally true of bishops and religious superiors who did not apply the law in force to bring offenders to justice within the Church.

The general procedure for responding to an accusation of the sexual abuse of a minor is defined in canon law. The procedure has been consistent for centuries, even if it was not followed in some cases, as we have now learned. An accusation is brought to the attention of the local bishop, who directs that a preliminary inquiry occur to determine if there is a foundation to the claim. Following this preliminary inquiry, unless it is clear that there is utterly no foundation, the bishop begins the process for conducting a full formal inquiry. This inquiry may be conducted through an administrative process, or through a judicial process (a trial). Throughout the last century, Church documents instructed bishops that a formal administrative or judicial process (a criminal trial conducted in the diocesan tribunal) was required to determine guilt or innocence.

By 2001 it had become clear that some bishops had not complied with the mandates in canon law to conduct the full inquiry, but instead had chosen to treat the sexual abuse of minors as a moral failing instead of a serious crime under canon law. Furthermore, because secrecy is a hallmark of this crime, an accusation by a victim or family member hardly gave rise in a bishop's mind to the thought that there were probably other victims, and perhaps many other victims.

Some bishops hoped that by transferring an offending priest, usually following psychiatric or psychological therapy and with the favorable recommendation of the therapist, the priest would be able to manage his illness in the same manner as an alcoholic, armed with increased insight into his vulnerabilities and with support from ongoing therapy or a twelve-step program. Some psychiatrists specializing in treating pedophilia recommended a course of therapy which included the regular injection of a medication, a hormone known as Depo-Provera. They suggested that this would reduce the libido and assist in managing sexual desires. Rather than choosing to punish a priest offender, some bishops preferred to extend mercy and the possibility of reform with careful management of the underlying disease under the care of psychiatric professionals.

This certainly proved to be the wrong approach, for it failed to recognize the seriousness of the addiction that defines pedophilia and ephebophilia, and it failed to consider the lingering and deeply traumatic effects of these acts on the victims. To be fair, although this proved to be tragically wrong, some bishops saw this response as a compassionate effort to provide assistance and opportunity for reform, based on unsound advice provided to them by medical and legal professionals. It cannot in every case rightly be characterized as a cover-up. It was, however, in every case a neglect of the Church's canon law, which demanded an inquiry and often a trial.

On April 30, 2001, Pope John Paul II promulgated the Apostolic Letter *Sacramentorum Sanctitatis Tutela* (often referred to by its initials only, *SST*), which updated in canon law the legal competence of the Vatican's Congregation for the Doctrine of the Faith over the investigation of the more serious delicts, or crimes against morals. The document was not a response to the emerging sexual abuse crisis. It was, rather, part of a lengthy and ongoing process of updating the procedures of the various Vatican offices. Its content was not new, but it repeated and reorganized the 1962 instruction to bishops on how to respond to these serious allegations. *SST* provided explicit norms which defined which more serious offenses (*graviora delicta* in Latin) fell within the exclusive competence of the Congregation for the Doctrine of the Faith. These included, among other particularly serious crimes, the sacramental absolution by a priest of a sexual partner, the solicitation to sexual acts made by a priest in the context or pretext of sacramental confession, and a sexual act by a cleric with a minor below the age of 18.

Canon 1395, §2 of the 1983 *Code of Canon Law* called for a just penalty for a cleric who sexually abused a minor below the age of 16. In order to parallel civil law, the bishops of the United States asked the Holy See for an abrogation, or modification, of the law for the dioceses of the United States. In 1994, the age was raised to 18, for a period of five years. In 1998, Pope John Paul II extended that change until April 2009. *SST* made this change permanent.

SST was certainly not the first legal text in the Church that targeted this crime as a major offense within the Church. Long before child sexual abuse was acknowledged as a societal problem affecting families and professions, the Church had for centuries recognized its moral and spiritual evils and proscribed it as a crime worthy of special attention and penalty. This recognition was updated four times in the twentieth century — in codes of canon law in 1917 and 1983, and in instructions to bishops issued in 1922 and 1962 — and it was brought into the new millennium by Pope John Paul II.

The 1917 *Code of Canon Law* was the first codified system of law for the Catholic Church. Its canon 2359, §2 clearly declared sexual activity by a cleric with a minor (younger than 16) as a delict or crime, and prescribed penalties up to and including dismissal from the clerical state. That canon lists legal sources for this prohibition going as far back as the *Decretum* of Gratian in the mid-eleventh century. Gratian's *Decretum* was itself not new, but was a compilation of existing laws, many going back to the earliest Christian centuries. The Church as a whole recognized and paid attention to the crime of sexual abuse of minors for many centuries, but unless an individual bishop chose to implement the law it was ineffective.

SST was an unmistakable indication of how seriously the Roman Pontiff and the Holy See considered both these acts themselves as well as the proper response to allegations concerning them. Norms were published by the Holy See in 2001 and amended in 2003 that implemented the provisions of *SST*. These norms directed that the results of the preliminary inquiry in each case were to be forwarded by the local bishop to the Congregation for the Doctrine of the Faith, which would direct the bishop whether to conduct a judicial or administrative process, or which would call the case to itself, to be heard in its own Supreme Tribunal of the Congregation for the Doctrine of the Faith. In practice as time went on, the Congregation also delegated or appointed tribunals in other dioceses to hear the case.

SST made mention of the 1962 Instruction, *Crimen sollicitationis*. That reference prompted many to search for the unpublished Instruction, which had typically been sent (in its original Latin) to bishops only when they reported a case to the Congregation, which was then known as the Congregation of the Holy Office. A faulty translation of that document came into the hands of the media in the early 2000's and made international headlines. This was reported as the "smoking gun" which proved that the Vatican had orchestrated a cover-up of sexual abuse cases. This fanciful claim was based on several misinterpretations of the document.

The document was, in fact, concerned with the proper procedure for bringing offenders to justice within the Church. It was entitled, "Instruction on the manner of proceeding in cases of solicitation," and as an Appendix it included 18 legal formularies to assist canon lawyers in drafting documents related to such cases. Although its principal topic was the proper means of responding to allegations of solicitation to sexual acts within the sacrament of Penance or confession, in Title V it spoke of the "worst sin" (*de crimine pessimo*), and restated that sexual activity with minors of either sex was not only gravely sinful but an ecclesiastical crime.

The Instruction did not provide new or additional procedures for handling a case of child sexual abuse, but referred ecclesiastical superiors to existing canon law procedures. Paragraph 74 of the Instruction directs bishops and religious superiors to conduct an inquiry according to existing administrative or judicial procedures, and to forward the results to the Holy Office. In all of this, the document repeated the dictates of the 1922 Instruction by the same name, which itself updated similar Vatican documents from past centuries. It should be noted that none of this was truly secret, since canon law texts and treatises concerning *de crimine pessimo* published in the mid-twentieth century routinely quoted verbatim from the 1922 Instruction.

SST also repeated an important provision of the related 1922 and 1962 documents, namely that cases of this nature are subject to "the pontifical secret." However, it is important to note that neither the 1922 nor the 1962 Instruction imposed "secrecy" in matters related to child sexual abuse. Rather, the secrecy was imposed on officials dealing with cases of solicitation to sexual acts in the confessional, and in no case was there a prohibition against reporting any crime to the public authorities.

Sadly, the notion of the pontifical secret has been seriously misunderstood and distorted in its interpretation. The official language of the Church is Latin, and some Latin legal terms do not translate easily into their English legal equivalents. The word "secret" is one of them, and so is the notion that an accusation is "reserved to the Holy See." In fact, there are three areas of common misunderstanding about how canon law treats the sexual abuse of minors by clerics: the notion of secrecy, the involvement of the Vatican, and the idea of "defrocking" a cleric.

What is the "pontifical secret"? In 1974, the Vatican's Secretariat of State published an Instruction, *Secreta continere*, in which this is discussed. It states that matters of major importance in the life of the Church require a strict level of confidentiality. The Latin word *secretum* poses a problem if it is uncritically transliterated into the English word "secret," because the English word carries connotations far beyond the meaning and purpose in canon law. No scholar of the law or of the Latin language would make such a mistake. The closest analog in English is "confidentiality," not "secret."

It is both unfortunate and unfair that the word "secret" has been uncritically employed to describe the confidentiality that is expected in response to allegations of the sexual abuse of a minor by a cleric. Instead of conveying the correct notion that the Church wants to protect the rights and reputations of all persons connected with such allegations, a poor translation may suggest that Church authorities use this legal mandate to cover up or deny them.

In truth, by imposing a high degree of confidentiality in these proceedings, the Church seeks to remove hindrances to a victim coming forward who might otherwise fear intimidation or public humiliation. Confidentiality is expected in criminal proceedings in most legal systems, to help protect the integrity of the process against those who might suborn perjury among witnesses, conspire to prevent the truth from being exposed, or intimidate witnesses or decision-makers. Lastly, victims seldom welcome the emotional trauma that comes with public discussion of their experiences.

"Reserved to the Holy See" is another problematic phrase for some. Unscrupulous critics of the Church see another way to cover up or hide a crime. The idea that a local bishop is bound to inform the Vatican about an accusation against a priest makes sense if one considers the global character of the Church. For Americans, it is roughly equivalent to declaring a crime a federal offense and insisting that it be tried in a federal court, removed from local interpretation or influences.

Why does this make sense? Until the most recent decades, nearly all canon lawyers were priests. It is possible that impartiality could be compromised if an accused cleric were brought to trial in the tribunal of his own diocese, where the judges are priests and perhaps friends of the accused. Similarly, a traumatized victim may not be comfortable giving testimony before other priests of the same diocese. Canon law has always permitted a trial regarding sexual abuse to be heard in Rome instead of locally. The Holy See maintains control over the response to so serious an accusation. A victim may fear that a local bishop would not take an accusation against one of his priests seriously, and so the Holy See must be involved in order to give the bishop some direction and to provide a safeguard against an overly lax approach.

Occasionally the Church is criticized for not having "defrocked" a cleric who sexually abused a minor. Some single-mindedly focus on this penalty as the only possible penalty, or as the most severe. It is one of several penalties available in canon law that have the necessary effect of removing an offending cleric from ministry, and in some cases it is not the most appropriate penalty.

As noted above, dismissal from the clerical state is an expiatory penalty, designed to punish a cleric guilty of a crime or serious offense. There are other expiatory penalties or punishments, however, and dismissal from the clerical state is not always the best or most severe penalty for a cleric. In a given set of circumstances, it is sometimes better to impose the penalty that a cleric — completely removed from any public ministry and with no faculties to serve as a priest — must live his days in prayer and penance for his past crime or crimes. In some situations this is a more effective preventative measure than dismissing him from ministry and losing all contact with him as he seeks other means of support. Daily, the priest is reminded of his victims as he prays for them and does penance for his sins. He is removed from public ministry and the Church can better ensure that his ability to contact minors is severely limited. If a priest is simply dismissed from the clerical state, he is often cut loose from any influence or restraint by the Church as he finds his own way in life. In each situation the cleric is completely removed from ministry, which fulfills a constant plea of victims: "Please don't let my abuser use his ministry as a means of ever hurting another child."

In sum, it is fair to say that the Catholic Church has long considered some behaviors to be offensive to good morals or the good order and Christian witness of the Church. Although the Church prefers to teach, and therefore to guide the formation of consciences, rather than to legislate moral action, there are some behaviors so offensive and hurtful that the Church declares them to be serious ecclesiastical offenses or crimes. By means of its canon law, the Church provides the mechanisms for responding to accusations of such hurtful behaviors, and also provides safeguards to ensure that the rights and reputations of victims and the accused are protected. It is tragic and scandalous that these mechanisms were not always observed or implemented by some bishops in past decades. Today there is a renewed awareness of a painful truth which the Church has long affirmed: that sinful acts may be more than moral transgressions. They may be criminal acts deserving of trial and punishment.

Guide to Understanding Basic CDF Procedures concerning Sexual Abuse Allegations

Released by the Vatican April 10, 2010

The applicable law is the *motu proprio Sacramentorum Sanctitatis Tutela* (MP *SST*) of 30 April 2001, together with the 1983 *Code of Canon Law*. This is an introductory guide which may be helpful to lay persons and noncanonists.

A: Preliminary Procedures

The local diocese investigates every allegation of sexual abuse of a minor by a cleric.

If the allegation has a semblance of truth, the case is referred to the CDF. The local bishop transmits all the necessary information to the CDF and expresses his opinion on the procedures to be followed and the measures to be adopted in the short and long term.

Civil law concerning reporting of crimes to the appropriate authorities should always be followed.

During the preliminary stage and until the case is concluded, the bishop may impose precautionary measures to safeguard the community, including the victims. Indeed, the local bishop always retains power to protect children by restricting the activities of any priest in his diocese. This is part of his ordinary authority, which he is encouraged to exercise to whatever extent is necessary to assure that children do not come to harm, and this power can be exercised at the bishop's discretion before, during, and after any canonical proceeding.

B: Procedures Authorized by the CDF

The CDF studies the case presented by the local bishop and also asks for supplementary information where necessary. The CDF has a number of options:

B1 Penal Processes

The CDF may authorize the local bishop to conduct a judicial penal trial before a local Church tribunal. Any appeal in such cases would eventually be lodged to a tribunal of the CDF.

The CDF may authorize the local bishop to conduct an administrative penal process before a delegate of the local bishop assisted by two assessors. The accused priest is called to respond to the accusations and to review the evidence. The accused has a right to present recourse to the CDF against a decree condemning him to a canonical penalty. The decision of the cardinal members of the CDF is final.

Should the cleric be judged guilty, both judicial and administrative penal processes can condemn a cleric to a number of canonical penalties, the most serious of which is dismissal from the clerical state. The question of damages can also be treated directly during these procedures.

B2 Cases referred directly to the Holy Father

In very grave cases where a civil criminal trial has found the cleric guilty of sexual abuse of minors or where the evidence is overwhelming, the CDF may choose to take the case directly to the Holy Father with the request that the pope issue a decree of "ex officio" dismissal from the clerical state. There is no canonical remedy against such a papal decree.

The CDF also brings to the Holy Father requests by accused priests who, cognizant of their crimes, ask to be dispensed from the obligation of the priesthood and want to return to the lay state. The Holy Father grants these requests for the good of the Church ("*pro bono Ecclesiae*").

B3 Disciplinary Measures

In cases where the accused priest has admitted to his crimes and has accepted to live a life of prayer and penance, the CDF authorizes the local bishop to issue a decree prohibiting or restricting the public ministry of such a priest. Such decrees are imposed through a penal precept which would entail a canonical penalty for a violation of the conditions of the decree, not excluding dismissal from the clerical state. Administrative recourse to the CDF is possible against such decrees. The decision of the CDF is final.

C. Revision of MP *SST*

For some time the CDF has undertaken a revision of some of the articles of Motu Proprio *Sacramentorum Sanctitatis Tutela*, in order to update the said Motu Proprio of 2001 in the light of special faculties granted to the CDF by Popes John Paul II and Benedict XVI. The proposed modifications under discussion will not change the above-mentioned procedures (A, B1-B3).

Statements and Commentary

Cardinal Joseph Ratzinger's Good Friday Meditations at the Stations of the Cross

As Pope John Paul II entered literally into the last weeks of his life, the pontiff's fragile condition made it necessary for the celebration of the liturgy of Good Friday to be entrusted into other hands. The choice fell to then-Cardinal Joseph Ratzinger who, in addition to being prefect of the Congregation for the Doctrine of the Faith, was also the Dean of the College of Cardinals, meaning he was the elected head of that body. The choice was a logical one, and the cardinal conducted what became one of the most memorable Good Friday liturgies in many years. It was so well remembered because of the meditations for the Stations of the Cross by Cardinal Ratzinger and also, most poignantly, the image of the frail John Paul watching on television in the papal apartment.

Cardinal Ratzinger used the wider theme of the Year of the Eucharist to focus on the Lord's words in the Gospel of John 12:24: "Unless a grain of wheat falls into the earth and dies, it remains alone; but if it dies, it bears much fruit." This served to ground his meditation in the Eucharist, and the cardinal mentioned in an interview with Vatican Radio that the Way of the Cross is more than a chain of suffering and terrible events. It is a mystery, the means by which the grain of wheat falls into the earth and bears fruit. In that sense, he declared, the Way of the Cross shows that the sacrifice of Christ bears fruit and becomes a gift for all. He proclaimed during the Way of the Cross, "The Lord compares the course of his whole earthly existence to that of a grain of wheat, which only by dying can produce fruit."

Cardinal Ratzinger paid special attention in the meditations on the three times that Christ falls on the way to Golgotha — the third, seventh, and ninth stations.

In the third station, he wrote:

> Man has fallen, and he continues to fall: often he becomes a caricature of himself, no longer the image of God, but a mockery of the Creator. . . . In Jesus' fall beneath the weight of the Cross, the meaning of his whole life is seen: his voluntary abasement, which lifts us up from the depths of our pride. The nature of our pride is also revealed: it is that arrogance which makes us want to be liberated from God and left alone to ourselves, the arrogance which makes us think that we do not need his eternal love, but can be the masters of our own lives.

In Jesus' second fall, the seventh station, Ratzinger cited the failings of Christians and ties them to the fall of Adam and the state of fallen humanity:

> In his First Letter, Saint John speaks of a threefold fall: lust of the flesh, lust of the eyes and the pride of life. He thus interprets the fall of man and humanity against the backdrop of the vices of his own time, with all its excesses and perversions. But we can also think, in more recent times, of how a Christianity which has grown weary of faith has abandoned the Lord: the great ideologies, and the banal existence of those who, no longer believing in anything, simply drift through life, have built a new and worse paganism, which in its attempt to do away with God once and for all, have ended up doing away with man.

This was merely the prelude to his final reflection, on Jesus' third fall, the ninth station. Here he charted the progression from "the fall of man in general [third station], and the falling of many Christians away from Christ and into a godless secularism [seventh station]" to the sorrow of "how much Christ suffers in his own Church." He provided a litany of the failings of those in the Church, and in his accompanying prayer, he cried out, "Lord, your Church often seems like a boat about to sink, a boat taking in water on every side. In your field we see more weeds than wheat."

Cardinal Ratzinger cited among the ills of the Church the falling of many Christians away from Christ and into a godless secularism, the abuse of the holy sacrament of his Presence, and how often Scripture is twisted and misused. But he saved his most stark criticism for unfaithful priests, above all those who are guilty of sexual abuse: "How much filth there is in the Church, and even among those who, in the priesthood, ought to belong entirely to him! How much pride, how much self-complacency!"

At the time, the comments during the Way of the Cross were seen as a vivid demonstration of Ratzinger's unhappiness with the sex abuse crisis and his determination to purify the Church and also seek a genuine renewal. There was also an obvious connection being made between the sex abuse crisis and the loss of faith. As he prayed at the end of his ninth meditation, "We can only call to him from the depths of our hearts: *Kyrie eleison* — Lord, save us (cf. *Mt* 8: 25)."

Way of the Cross at the Colosseum
Good Friday 2005

Meditations and Prayers by Cardinal Joseph Ratzinger

[excerpt]

THIRD STATION
Jesus falls for the first time

V/. *Adoramus te, Christe, et benedicimus tibi.*
R/. *Quia per sanctam crucem tuam redemisti mundum.*

From the Book of the Prophet Isaiah. 53:4-6

Surely he has borne our griefs and carried our sorrows; yet we esteemed him stricken, smitten by God, and afflicted. But he was wounded for our transgressions, he was bruised for our iniquities; upon him was the chastisement that made us whole, and with his stripes we are healed. All we like sheep have gone astray; we have turned every one to his own way; and the LORD has laid on him the iniquity of us all.

Meditation

Man has fallen, and he continues to fall: often he becomes a caricature of himself, no longer the image of God, but a mockery of the Creator. Is not the man who, on the way from Jerusalem to Jericho, fell among robbers who stripped him and left him half-dead and bleeding beside the road, the image of humanity par excellence? Jesus' fall beneath the Cross is not just the fall of the man Jesus, exhausted from his scourging. There is a more profound meaning in this fall, as Paul tells us in the Letter to the Philippians: "Though he was in the form of God, he did not count equality with God a thing to be grasped, but emptied himself, taking the form of a servant, being born in the likeness of men. . . . he humbled himself and became obedient unto death, even death on a cross" (*Phil* 2:6-8). In Jesus' fall beneath the weight of the Cross, the meaning of his whole life is seen: his voluntary abasement, which lifts us up from the depths of our pride. The nature of our pride is also revealed: it is that arrogance which makes us want to be liberated from God and left alone to ourselves, the arrogance which makes us think that we do not need his eternal love, but can be the masters of our own lives. In this rebellion against truth, in this attempt to be our own god, creator and judge, we fall headlong and plunge into self-destruction. The humility of Jesus is the surmounting of our pride; by his abasement he lifts us up. Let us allow him to lift us up. Let us strip away our sense of self-sufficiency, our false illusions of independence, and learn from him, the One who humbled himself, to discover our true greatness by bending low before God and before our downtrodden brothers and sisters.

[. . .]

SEVENTH STATION
Jesus falls for the second time

V/. *Adoramus te, Christe, et benedicimus tibi.*
R/. *Quia per sanctam crucem tuam redemisti mundum.*

From the Book of Lamentations. 3:1-2, 9, 16

I am the man who has seen affliction under the rod of his wrath; he has driven and brought me into darkness without any light. He has blocked my ways with hewn stones, he has made my paths crooked. He has made my teeth grind on gravel, and made me cower in ashes.

Meditation

The tradition that Jesus fell three times beneath the weight of the Cross evokes the fall of Adam, the state of fallen humanity, and the mystery of Jesus' own sharing in our fall. Throughout history, the fall of man constantly takes on new forms. In his First Letter, Saint John speaks of a threefold fall: lust of the flesh, lust of the eyes and the pride of life. He thus interprets the fall of man and humanity against the backdrop of the vices of his own time, with all its excesses and perversions. But we can also think, in more recent times, of how a Christianity which has grown weary of faith has abandoned the Lord: the great ideologies, and the banal existence of those who, no longer believing in anything, simply drift through life, have built a new and worse paganism, which in its attempt to do away with God once and for all, have ended up doing away with man. And so man lies fallen in the dust. The Lord bears this burden and falls, over and over again, in order to meet us. He gazes on us, he touches our hearts; he falls in order to raise us up.

NINTH STATION
Jesus falls for the third time

V/. *Adoramus te, Christe, et benedicimus tibi.*
R/. *Quia per sanctam crucem tuam redemisti mundum.*

From the Book of Lamentations. 3:27-32

It is good for a man that he bear the yoke in his youth. Let him sit alone in silence when he has laid it on him; let him put his mouth in the dust — there may yet be hope; let him give his cheek to the smiter, and be filled with insults. For the Lord will not cast off for ever, but, though he cause grief, he will have compassion, according to the abundance of his steadfast love.

Meditation

What can the third fall of Jesus under the Cross say to us? We have considered the fall of man in general, and the falling of many Christians away from Christ and into a godless secularism. Should we not also think of how much Christ suffers in his own Church? How often is the holy sacrament of his Presence abused, how often must he enter empty and evil hearts! How often do we celebrate only ourselves, without even realizing that he is there! How often is his Word twisted and misused! What little faith is present behind so many theories, so many empty words! How much filth there is in the Church, and even among those who, in the priesthood, ought to belong entirely to him! How much pride, how much self-complacency! What little respect we pay to the Sacrament of Reconciliation, where he waits for us, ready to raise us up whenever we fall! All this is present in his Passion. His betrayal by his disciples, their unworthy reception of his Body and Blood, is certainly the greatest suffering endured by the Redeemer; it pierces his heart. We can only call to him from the depths of our hearts: *Kyrie eleison* — Lord, save us (cf. *Mt* 8:25).

Pope Benedict XVI's *Ad Limina* address to the Irish bishops

A year and a half after becoming pope, Benedict XVI welcomed to the Vatican the bishops of Ireland who were making the required five year visit to the Holy See by all bishops, the so-called *ad limina*. The event provided the Holy Father with his first major opportunity to address the issue of sex abuse since his memorable comments prior to his election as pope. It was also his first chance to speak about the problems confronting the Irish Church. In attendance was virtually the whole of the Irish hierarchy, including several bishops who went on to resign in the aftermath of the Murphy and Ryan Reports of 2009 that detailed the scale of the history of sexual and physical abuse by some Catholic and religious priests across Ireland.

At the time of the *ad limina* visit, the Irish bishops were already under intense scrutiny for the wave of cases that had come to light in the previous years. While the cases had taken place in the past, the failures of the Church's leadership and also civil authorities were coming into focus thanks to the details that were emerging. These were revealed shockingly in the Murphy and Ryan Reports of 2009.

The mood was grim when the bishops gathered to meet with the pope on October 28, and the pontiff's reflections were at times blunt. After acknowledging the contributions of Irish culture and faith to the life of the Church, "and the extraordinary courage of her missionary sons and daughters who have carried the Gospel message far beyond her shores," he expressed his immense sadness for the toll of the scandals that have struck the Irish Church, the suffering of the victims, and the state of Irish culture which has been under attack for many years from the challenges of secularism, materialism and modernity. He described the cases as "heart-rending," and added that they "are all the more tragic when the abuser is a cleric."

The *ad limina* address anticipated some of the major themes that have been established as cornerstones of moving forward. He noted, "It is an urgent task to rebuild confidence and trust where these have been damaged." He then added the importance of establishing the truth of what happened in the past, but made the key distinction that the bishops must build on this "to take whatever steps are necessary to prevent it from occurring again, to ensure that the principles of justice are fully respected and, above all, to bring healing to the victims and to all those affected by these egregious crimes."

The pope moved on to speak to the priests and religious of Ireland who have also been impacted so negatively by the scandals: "The fine work and selfless dedication of the great majority of priests and religious in Ireland should not be obscured by the transgressions of some of their brethren."

Related to this was the issue of vocations, and the pope acknowledged the drastic drop in seminarians in the last decade. He lamented, "At one time, Ireland was blessed with such an abundance of priestly and religious vocations that much of the world was able to benefit from their apostolic labors. In recent years, though, the number of vocations has fallen sharply." He encouraged the Irish bishops in their quest to increase vocations and expressed his pleasure that included in that effort is the practice of silent prayer for vocations before the Blessed Sacrament."

He then spoke of the young people, whose faith has been so tried by the scandals but who remain spiritually hungry.

Within that context, he recognized the associated problem that the religious life and commitment to the Christian journey had become unfashionable in Ireland.

Address of His Holiness Benedict XVI to the Bishops of Ireland on their *Ad Limina* visit Consistory Hall, Saturday, October 28, 2006

Dear Brother Bishops,

In the words of a traditional Irish greeting, a hundred thousand welcomes to you, the Bishops of Ireland, on the occasion of your *ad Limina* visit. As you venerate the tombs of the Apostles Peter and Paul, may you draw inspiration from the courage and vision of these two great saints, who so faithfully led the way in the Church's mission of proclaiming Christ to the world. Today you have come to strengthen the bonds of communion with the Successor of Peter, and I gladly express my appreciation for the gracious words addressed to me on your behalf by Archbishop Seán Brady, President of your Episcopal Conference. The constant witness of countless generations of Irish people to their faith in Christ and their fidelity to the Holy See has shaped Ireland at the deepest level of her history and culture. We are all aware of the outstanding contribution that Ireland has made to the life of the Church, and the extraordinary courage of her missionary sons and daughters who have carried the Gospel message far beyond her shores. Meanwhile, the flame of faith has continued bravely burning at home through all the trials afflicting your people in the course of their history. In the words of the Psalmist, "I will sing of thy steadfast love, O LORD, for ever; with my mouth I will proclaim thy faithfulness to all generations" (*Ps* 89:1).

The present time brings many new opportunities to bear witness to Christ and fresh challenges for the Church in

Ireland. You have spoken about the consequences for society of the rise in prosperity that the last fifteen years have brought. After centuries of emigration, which involved the pain of separation for so many families, you are experiencing for the first time a wave of immigration. Traditional Irish hospitality is finding unexpected new outlets. Like the wise householder who brings forth from his treasure "what is new and what is old" (*Mt* 13:52), your people need to view the changes in society with discernment, and here they look to you for leadership. Help them to recognize the inability of the secular, materialist culture to bring true satisfaction and joy. Be bold in speaking to them of the joy that comes from following Christ and living according to his commandments. Remind them that our hearts were made for the Lord and that they find no peace until they rest in him (cf. Saint Augustine, *Confessions*, 1:1).

So often the Church's counter-cultural witness is misunderstood as something backward and negative in today's society. That is why it is important to emphasize the Good News, the life-giving and life-enhancing message of the Gospel (cf. *Jn* 10:10). Even though it is necessary to speak out strongly against the evils that threaten us, we must correct the idea that Catholicism is merely "a collection of prohibitions". Sound catechesis and careful "formation of the heart" are needed here, and in this regard you are blessed in Ireland with solid resources in your network of Catholic schools, and in so many dedicated religious and lay teachers who are seriously committed to the education of the young. Continue to encourage them in their task and ensure that their catechetical programs are based on the *Catechism of the Catholic Church*, as well as the new *Compendium*. Superficial presentations of Catholic teaching must be avoided, because only the fullness of the faith can communicate the liberating power of the Gospel. By exercising vigilance over the quality of the syllabuses and the course-books used and by proclaiming the Church's doctrine in its entirety, you are carrying out your responsibility to "preach the word . . . in season and out of season . . . unfailing in patience and in teaching" (2 Tim 4:2).

In the exercise of your pastoral ministry, you have had to respond in recent years to many heart-rending cases of sexual abuse of minors. These are all the more tragic when the abuser is a cleric. The wounds caused by such acts run deep, and it is an urgent task to rebuild confidence and trust where these have been damaged. In your continuing efforts to deal effectively with this problem, it is important to establish the truth of what happened in the past, to take whatever steps are necessary to prevent it from occurring again, to ensure that the principles of justice are fully respected and, above all, to bring healing to the victims and to all those affected by these egregious crimes. In this way, the Church in Ireland will grow stronger and be ever more capable of giving witness to the redemptive power of the Cross of Christ. I pray that by the grace of the Holy Spirit, this time of purification will enable all God's people in Ireland to "maintain and perfect in their lives that holiness which they have received from God" (Lumen Gentium, 40).

The fine work and selfless dedication of the great majority of priests and religious in Ireland should not be obscured by the transgressions of some of their brethren. I am certain that the people understand this, and continue to regard their clergy with affection and esteem. Encourage your priests always to seek spiritual renewal and to discover afresh the joy of ministering to their flocks within the great family of the Church. At one time, Ireland was blessed with such an abundance of priestly and religious vocations that much of the world was able to benefit from their apostolic labors. In recent years, though, the number of vocations has fallen sharply. How urgent it is, then, to heed the Lord's words: "The harvest is plentiful, but the laborers are few. Pray, therefore, the Lord of the harvest to send out laborers into his harvest" (Mt 9:37-38). I am pleased to learn that many of your dioceses have adopted the practice of silent prayer for vocations before the Blessed Sacrament. This should be warmly encouraged. Yet above all, it falls to you, the Bishops, and to your clergy to offer young people an inspiring and attractive vision of the ordained priesthood. Our prayer for vocations "must lead to action so that from our praying heart a spark of our joy in God and in the Gospel may arise, enkindling in the hearts of others a readiness to say 'yes'" (*Address to Priests and Permanent Deacons*, Freising, 14 September 2006). Even if Christian commitment is considered unfashionable in some circles, there is a real spiritual hunger and a generous desire to serve others among the young people of Ireland. A vocation to the priesthood or the religious life offers an opportunity to respond to this desire in a way that brings deep joy and personal fulfillment.

Allow me to add an observation that is close to my heart. For many years, Christian representatives of all denominations, political leaders and many men and women of good will have been involved in seeking means to ensure a brighter future for Northern Ireland. Although the path is arduous, much progress has been made in recent times. It is my prayer that the committed efforts of those concerned will lead to the creation of a society marked by a spirit of reconciliation, mutual respect and willing cooperation for the common good of all.

As you prepare to return to your dioceses, I commend your apostolic ministry to the intercession of all the saints of Ireland, and I assure you of my deep affection and constant prayer for you and for the Irish people. May Our Lady of Knock watch over and protect you always. To all of you, and to the priests, religious and lay faithful of your beloved island I cordially impart my Apostolic Blessing as a pledge of peace and joy in the Lord Jesus Christ.

Pope Benedict XVI's in-flight press conference on his way to the United States

From April 15 to 21, 2008, Pope Benedict XVI visited Washington, D.C., and New York to mark the occasion of the 200th anniversary of the declaration of Baltimore as the first metropolitan see of the United States and the creation of the suffragan sees Bardstown (Kentucky), Boston, New York, and Philadelphia. The pontiff also visited the United Nations.

The papal visit was the first for the pontiff to the U.S. since his election in April 2005; prior to his election then-Cardinal Joseph Ratzinger had been to the United States several times and expressed great fondness for the country. The remarkable achievements of the United States were mentioned several times by the pope, and the trip allowed the Holy Father to make direct contact with Americans and American Catholics and to give expression to the theme, "Christ Our Hope." The theme was reiterated throughout his homilies and speeches.

Pope Benedict was received with genuine enthusiasm and great affection in both Washington and New York, and his presence and teachings were considered timely and important for Catholics in the United States. Despite being elected three years before and entering the papacy as one of the best-known cardinals of the late twentieth century, the pontiff was unfamiliar to most Americans (and American Catholics in particular) who had heard only of his work as head of the Congregation for the Doctrine of the Faith or as a "conservative" theologian. In the lead-up to the visit, American media speculated intensely on whether and how the pontiff would deal with the issue of the sex-abuse scandal that created such a severe crisis for the Church in the United States from 2002. The media were thus taken entirely by surprise when Pope Benedict addressed the issue directly on the flight from Italy to Washington.

The first question on the flight was asked by the American journalist John Allen and related to the sexual abuse crisis.

The answer of Pope Benedict was succinct, but he accomplished several important objectives. First, he announced that the issue of the sexual abuse crisis was not going to be given little attention or that it was some mere afterthought. It was the first major topic of discussion for the pope and remained so throughout the visit.

Second, the pontiff established a willingness to speak in unmistakable terms of penance for the Church. He says plainly, "I am ashamed and we will do everything possible to ensure that this does not happen in [the] future."

The pope then detailed a threefold plan for dealing with the crisis: a concern for justice; helping victims to receive healing; and the need for institutional reform.

Interview of the Holy Father Benedict XVI during the flight to the United States of America
Tuesday, April 15, 2008

[*excerpt*]

Fr. Lombardi: Welcome, Your Holiness! In the name of all my colleagues present, I thank you for your gracious availability in giving us suggestions and ideas for reporting on this journey. It is your second intercontinental trip: your first as Pope

to America, to the United States and to the United Nations. It
is an important and eagerly-awaited visit. To begin with, could
you tell us something about how you feel, the hopes you have
for this journey and what is its fundamental goal from your
viewpoint?

The Holy Father: My journey has two goals in particular. The first is to visit the Church in America, in the United
States. There is one special reason for it: 200 years ago Baltimore was raised to a Metropolitan See and at the same time
four other new dioceses came into being: New York, Philadelphia, Boston, and Louisville. Thus, it is a great Jubilee for this
core of the Church in the United States, a time of reflection
on the past and above all of reflection on the future, on how
to respond to the great challenges of our time, in the present and in view of the future. And naturally, interreligious
and ecumenical meetings are part of this Visit, especially an
additional Meeting in the Synagogue with our Jewish friends
on the eve of their Passover Feast. This is, therefore, the religious and pastoral aspect of the Church in the United States
at this moment in our history, and the Meeting with all the
others in this common brotherhood that binds us in a common
responsibility. At this time I would also like to thank President
Bush who will be at the airport to meet me and set aside a lot
of time for conversation, besides receiving me on my birthday.
The second goal is the Visit to the United Nations. Here too
there is a special reason: 60 years have passed since the Universal Declaration of Human Rights. This is the anthropological
basis, the philosophy, on which the United Nations stands, the
human and spiritual foundations on which it is built. Thus, it is
truly a time for reflection, the time to resume awareness of this
important stage in history. Various different cultural traditions
converged in the Declaration of Human Rights, above all, an
anthropology that recognizes man as a subject of rights preced-
ing all institutions, with common values to be respected by all.

This Visit, which is taking place precisely at the moment of a crisis in values, therefore seems to me to be important in order to reconfirm together that everything began at that moment and to recover it for our future.

Fr. Lombardi: Let us now move on to the questions that you presented in the past few days and that some of you will present to the Holy Father. Let us begin with the question of John Allen, whom I do not think needs to be introduced since he is a very well known commentator on Vatican affairs in the United States.

Holy Father, I am asking the question in English, if I may, and perhaps, if it were possible, if we could have a sentence or a word in English we would be very grateful. This is the question: the Church you will find in the United States is a large Church, a lively Church, but also a suffering Church, in a certain sense, especially because of the recent crisis caused by sexual abuse. The American people are expecting a word from you, a message from you on this crisis. What will be your message for this suffering Church?

The Holy Father (in English): It is a great suffering for the Church in the United States and for the Church in general, for me personally, that this could happen. If I read the history of these events, it is difficult for me to understand how it was possible for priests to fail in this way in the mission to give healing, to give God's love to these children. I am ashamed and we will do everything possible to ensure that this does not happen in future. I think we have to act on three levels: the first is at the level of justice and the political level. I will not speak at this moment about homosexuality: this is another thing. We will absolutely exclude pedophiles from the sacred ministry; it is absolutely incompatible, and whoever is really guilty of being a pedophile cannot be a priest. So at this first level we can do justice and help the victims, because they are deeply affected; these are the two sides of justice: one, that pedophiles cannot be priests and the other, to help in any possible way the victims. Then there is a pastoral level. The victims will need healing and help and assistance and reconciliation: this is a big pastoral engagement and I know that the Bishops and the priests and all Catholic people in the United States will do whatever possible to help, to assist, to heal. We have made a visitation of the seminaries and we will do all that is possible in the education of seminarians for a deep spiritual, human and intellectual formation for the students. Only sound persons can be admitted to the priesthood and only persons with a deep personal life in Christ and who have a deep sacramental life. So, I know that the Bishops and directors of seminarians will do all possible to have a strong, strong discernment because it is more important to have good priests than to have many priests. This is also our third level, and we hope that we can do, and have done and will do in the future, all that is possible to heal these wounds.

Pope Benedict XVI's address to the bishops of the United States at the Basilica of the National Shrine of the Immaculate Conception

The in-flight press conference and the attention paid to the sex abuse scandal, even before the start of events in Washington, D.C., was an indication of papal attention to the problem. As events transpired, the Holy Father addressed the crisis several more times during his American tour. One of the most significant was an unannounced meeting with four sex abuse victims from the archdiocese of Boston at the apostolic nunciature in Washington.

The next papal declaration came during the celebration of vespers and a meeting with the bishops of the United States of America at the National Shrine of the Immaculate Conception in Washington on April 16.

The pontiff spoke on several key themes, from the diverse origins of the Church in American Catholic history to the dangers of modern materialism and prosperity on families, to the abiding historical faith and charity of the American people. As his audience was the American hierarchy, Pope Benedict focused on the duties and obligations of bishops and reminded them that they "are called to sow the seeds of the Gospel today."

In this regard, he addressed the risks posed by "the subtle influence of secularism" and asked if it is "consistent to profess our beliefs in church on Sunday, and then during the week to promote business practices or medical procedures contrary to those beliefs? Is it consistent for practicing Catholics to ignore or exploit the poor and the marginalized, to promote sexual behavior contrary to Catholic moral teaching, or to adopt positions that contradict the right to life of every human being from conception to natural death?" He added to this the dangers posed by "the subtle influence of materialism" and the way that people can "lose sight of our dependence on others as well as the responsibilities that we bear towards them."

He lauded the blessing of a diverse Catholic laity who places its many gifts at the service of both the Church and society. But this blessing is attended by the need to maintain carefully the emphasis on religious education for children and adults. Likewise, the pope called on the bishops "to participate in the exchange of ideas in the public square, helping to shape cultural attitudes."

The role of the Church that is entrusted to the bishops is the state of the family within society. He told the bishops, "It is your task to proclaim boldly the arguments from faith and reason in favor of the institution of marriage, understood as a lifelong commitment between a man and a woman, open to the transmission of life."

These topics served as the introduction to Pope Benedict's concern with the sex abuse crisis, which took up nearly a third of the overall address to the bishops. As he did in his in-flight press conference, the pontiff used the word "shame" and again hit the themes that were first developed briefly on his way to the United States. Here he centered his concern on the role of the bishops in solving this crisis and the importance on the part of the bishops "to bind up the wounds caused by every breach of trust, to foster healing, to promote reconciliation and to reach out with loving concern to those so seriously wronged."

Celebration of Vespers and Meeting with the Bishops of the United States of America Address of His Holiness Benedict XVI National Shrine of the Immaculate Conception in Washington, DC, Wednesday, April 16, 2008

[excerpt]

Dear Brother Bishops,

It gives me great joy to greet you today, at the start of my visit to this country, and I thank Cardinal George for the gracious words he has addressed to me on your behalf. I want to thank all of you, especially the Officers of the Episcopal Conference, for the hard work that has gone into the preparation of this visit. My grateful appreciation goes also to the staff and volunteers of the National Shrine, who have welcomed us here this evening. American Catholics are noted for their loyal devotion to the See of Peter. My pastoral visit here is an opportunity to strengthen further the bonds of communion that unite us. We began by celebrating Evening Prayer in this Basilica dedicated to the Immaculate Conception of the Blessed Virgin Mary, a shrine of special significance to American Catholics, right in the heart of your capital city. Gathered in prayer with Mary, Mother of Jesus, we lovingly commend to our heavenly Father the people of God in every part of the United States.

For the Catholic communities of Boston, New York, Philadelphia, and Louisville, this is a year of particular celebration, as it marks the bicentenary of the establishment of these local Churches as dioceses. I join you in giving thanks for the many graces granted to the Church there during these two centuries. As this year also marks the bicentenary of the elevation of the founding see of Baltimore to an archdiocese, it gives me an opportunity to recall with admiration and gratitude the life and ministry of John Carroll, the first Bishop of Baltimore — a worthy leader of the Catholic community in your newly independent nation. His tireless efforts to spread the Gospel in the vast territory under his care laid the foundations for the ecclesial life of your country and enabled the Church in America to grow to maturity. Today the Catholic community you serve is one of the largest in the world, and one of the most influential. How important it is, then, to let your light so shine before your fellow citizens and before the world, "that they may see your good works and give glory to your Father who is in heaven" (*Mt* 5:16).

[. . .]

As my predecessor, Pope John Paul II, taught, "The person principally responsible in the diocese for the pastoral care of the family is the Bishop . . . he must devote to it personal interest, care, time, personnel and resources, but above all personal support for the families and for all those who . . . assist him in the pastoral care of the family" (*Familiaris Consortio*, 73). It is your task to proclaim boldly the arguments from faith and reason in favor of the institution of marriage, understood as a lifelong commitment between a man and a woman, open to the transmission of life. This message should resonate with people today, because it is essentially an unconditional and unreserved "yes" to life, a "yes" to love, and a "yes" to the aspirations at the heart of our common humanity, as we strive to fulfill our deep yearning for intimacy with others and with the Lord.

Among the countersigns to the Gospel of life found in America and elsewhere is one that causes deep shame: the sexual abuse of minors. Many of you have spoken to me of the enormous pain that your communities have suffered when clerics have betrayed their priestly obligations and duties by such gravely immoral behavior. As you strive to eliminate this evil wherever it occurs, you may be assured of the prayerful support of God's people throughout the world. Rightly, you attach priority to showing compassion and care to the victims. It is your God-given responsibility as pastors to bind up the wounds caused by every breach of trust, to foster healing, to promote reconciliation and to reach out with loving concern to those so seriously wronged.

Responding to this situation has not been easy and, as the President of your Episcopal Conference has indicated, it was "sometimes very badly handled". Now that the scale and gravity of the problem is more clearly understood, you have been able to adopt more focused remedial and disciplinary measures and to promote a safe environment that gives greater protection to young people. While it must be remembered that the overwhelming majority of clergy and religious in America do outstanding work in bringing the liberating message of the Gospel to the people entrusted to their care, it is vitally important that the vulnerable always be shielded from those who would cause harm. In this regard, your efforts to heal and protect are bearing great fruit not only for those directly under your pastoral care, but for all of society.

If they are to achieve their full purpose, however, the policies and programs you have adopted need to be placed in a wider context. Children deserve to grow up with a healthy understanding of sexuality and its proper place in human relationships. They should be spared the degrading manifestations and the crude manipulation of sexuality so prevalent today. They have a right to be educated in authentic moral values rooted in the dignity of the human person. This brings us back to our consideration of the centrality of the family and the need to promote the Gospel of life. What does it mean to speak of child protection when pornography and violence can be viewed in so many homes through media widely available today? We need to reassess urgently the values underpinning society, so that a sound moral formation can be offered to young people and adults alike. All have a part to play in this task — not only parents, religious leaders, teachers and catechists, but the media and entertainment industries as well. Indeed, every member of society can contribute to this moral renewal and benefit from it. Truly caring about young people and the future of our civilization means recognizing our responsibility to promote and live by the authentic moral values which alone enable the human person to flourish. It falls to you, as pastors modeled upon Christ, the Good Shepherd, to proclaim this message loud and clear, and thus to address the sin of abuse within the wider context of sexual *mores*. Moreover, by acknowledging and confronting the problem when it occurs in an ecclesial setting, you can give a lead to others, since this scourge is found not only within your dioceses but in every sector of society. It calls for a determined, collective response.

Priests, too, need your guidance and closeness during this difficult time. They have experienced shame over what has occurred, and there are those who feel they have lost some of the trust and esteem they once enjoyed. Not a few are experiencing a closeness to Christ in his Passion as they struggle to come to terms with the consequences of the crisis. The Bishop, as father, brother, and friend of his priests, can help them to draw spiritual fruit from this union with Christ by making them aware of the Lord's consoling presence in the midst of their suffering, and by encouraging them to walk with the Lord along the path of hope (cf. *Spe Salvi*, 39). As Pope John Paul II observed six years ago, "We must be confident that this time of trial will bring a purification of the entire Catholic community", leading to "a holier priesthood, a holier episcopate and a holier Church" (*Address to the Cardinals of the United States*, 23 April 2002, 4). There are many signs that, during the intervening period, such purification has indeed been taking place. Christ's abiding presence in the midst of our suffering is gradually transforming our darkness into light: all things are indeed being made new in Christ Jesus our hope.

At this stage a vital part of your task is to strengthen relationships with your clergy, especially in those cases where tension has arisen between priests and their bishops in the wake of the crisis. It is important that you continue to show them your concern, to support them, and to lead by example. In this way you will surely help them to encounter the living God, and point them towards the life-transforming hope of which the Gospel speaks. If you yourselves live in a manner closely configured to Christ, the Good Shepherd, who laid down his life for his sheep, you will inspire your brother priests to rededicate themselves to the service of their flocks with Christ-like generosity. Indeed a clearer focus upon the imitation of Christ in holiness of life is exactly what is needed in order for us to move forward. We need to rediscover the joy of living a Christ-centered life, cultivating the virtues, and immersing ourselves in prayer. When the faithful know that their pastor is a man who prays and who dedicates his life to serving them, they respond with warmth and affection, which nourishes and sustains the life of the whole community.

Time spent in prayer is never wasted, however urgent the duties that press upon us from every side. Adoration of Christ our Lord in the Blessed Sacrament prolongs and intensifies the union with him that is established through the Eucharistic celebration (cf. *Sacramentum Caritatis*, 66). Contemplation of the mysteries of the Rosary releases all their saving power and it conforms, unites and consecrates us to Jesus Christ (cf. *Rosarium Virginis Mariae*, 11, 15). Fidelity to the Liturgy of the Hours ensures that the whole of our day is sanctified and it continually reminds us of the need to remain focused on doing God's work, however many pressures and distractions may arise from the task at hand. Thus our devotion helps us to speak and act *in persona Christi*, to teach, govern and sanctify the faithful in the name of Jesus, to bring his reconciliation, his healing and his love to all his beloved brothers and sisters.

This radical configuration to Christ, the Good Shepherd, lies at the heart of our pastoral ministry, and if we open ourselves through prayer to the power of the Spirit, he will give us the gifts we need to carry out our daunting task, so that we need never "be anxious how to speak or what to say" (*Mt* 10:19).

Pope Benedict XVI's homily at the Mass at the Washington Nationals Stadium

The day after his address to the bishops of the United States, Pope Benedict celebrated a colorful Mass at Washington Nationals Stadium in Washington, D.C. He delivered a homily that extolled the faith and hope that had been a hallmark of the life of the Church in the United States since the first arrival of the Catholic faith in North America and added that one can praise the diversity of the Church, the common commitment to the Gospel and the awareness of the importance of the human person. The country, however, must now look forward to the future, "firmly grounded in the faith passed on by previous generations, and ready to meet new challenges."

He then placed this growth of the Catholic faith in America within the legacy of the Church's expansion after Pentecost and the way that the Church is called "to grow in unity through constant conversion to Christ" which, "in turn, gives rise to an unceasing missionary outreach."

In that regard, he warned that the Church in America and society as well stand at crossroads. He enumerated the threats we are facing: "signs of alienation, anger and polarization on the part of many of our contemporaries; increased violence; a weakening of the moral sense; a coarsening of social relations; and a growing forgetfulness of Christ and God." These dangers extend to the Church as well.

The solution to these dangers is "Christ Our Hope," and Benedict noted Americans have always been a people of hope, even if there have been many in the country who have not shared fully in that promise. "Yet hope," the pontiff stressed, "hope for the future, is very much a part of the American character."

It was the very notion of hope that served for Benedict as the introduction to the sexual abuse crisis.

Faithful to his theme of pastoral care for the victims, Benedict began his discussion of the crisis in the homily by acknowledging the pain and then proceeded to describe that "efforts have already been made to deal honestly and fairly with this tragic situation, and to ensure that children — whom our Lord loves so deeply (cf. *Mk* 10:14), and who are our greatest treasure — can grow up in a safe environment."

He then encouraged every Catholic "to do what you can to foster healing and reconciliation, and to assist those who have been hurt." Finally, returning to another theme, he pleaded for Catholics to love their priests and to affirm them in their labors.

From this direct reference, the pope moved on to the role of conversion and fidelity to the Gospel. Christ entrusted to the Apostles the authority to forgive sin, and this power has been entrusted to what Benedict termed "frail human ministers." Through Christ's grace, entrusted to these ministers, "the Church is constantly reborn and each of us is given the hope of a new beginning." This means the use of the sacrament of Penance, and he warned that "the renewal of the Church in America and throughout the world depends on the renewal of the practice of Penance and the growth in holiness which that sacrament both inspires and accomplishes."

Holy Mass
Homily of His Holiness Benedict XVI
Washington Nationals Stadium
Thursday, April 17, 2008

[excerpt]

Our Mass today brings the Church in the United States back to its roots in nearby Maryland, and commemorates the bicentennial of the first chapter of its remarkable growth — the division by my predecessor, Pope Pius VII, of the original diocese of Baltimore and the establishment of the dioceses of Boston, Bardstown (now Louisville), New York, and Philadelphia. Two hundred years later, the Church in America can rightfully praise the accomplishment of past generations in bringing together widely differing immigrant groups within the unity of the Catholic faith and in a common commitment to the spread of the Gospel. At the same time, conscious of its rich diversity, the Catholic community in this country has come to appreciate ever more fully the importance of each individual and group offering its own particular gifts to the whole. The Church in the United States is now called to look to the future, firmly grounded in the faith passed on by previous generations, and ready to meet new challenges — challenges no less demanding than those faced by your forebears — with the hope born of God's love, poured into our hearts by the Holy Spirit (cf. *Rom* 5:5).

In the exercise of my ministry as the Successor of Peter, I have come to America to confirm you, my brothers and sisters, in the faith of the Apostles (cf. *Lk* 22:32). I have come to proclaim anew, as Peter proclaimed on the day of Pentecost, that Jesus Christ is Lord and Messiah, risen from the dead, seated in glory at the right hand of the Father, and established as judge of the living and the dead (cf. *Acts* 2:14ff.). I have come to

repeat the Apostle's urgent call to conversion and the forgiveness of sins, and to implore from the Lord a new outpouring of
the Holy Spirit upon the Church in this country. As we have
heard throughout this Easter season, the Church was born of
the Spirit's gift of repentance and faith in the risen Lord. In
every age she is impelled by the same Spirit to bring to men
and women of every race, language, and people (cf. *Rev* 5:9)
the good news of our reconciliation with God in Christ.

[. . .]

Dear friends, my visit to the United States is meant to be
a witness to "Christ our Hope". Americans have always been
a people of hope: your ancestors came to this country with the
expectation of finding new freedom and opportunity, while
the vastness of the unexplored wilderness inspired in them the
hope of being able to start completely anew, building a new
nation on new foundations. To be sure, this promise was not
experienced by all the inhabitants of this land; one thinks of the
injustices endured by the native American peoples and by those
brought here forcibly from Africa as slaves. Yet hope, hope for
the future, is very much a part of the American character. And
the Christian virtue of hope — the hope poured into our hearts
by the Holy Spirit, the hope which supernaturally purifies and
corrects our aspirations by focusing them on the Lord and his
saving plan — that hope has also marked, and continues to
mark, the life of the Catholic community in this country.

It is in the context of this hope, born of God's love and fidelity, that I acknowledge the pain which the Church in America
has experienced as a result of the sexual abuse of minors. No
words of mine could describe the pain and harm inflicted by
such abuse. It is important that those who have suffered be
given loving pastoral attention. Nor can I adequately describe
the damage that has occurred within the community of the
Church. Great efforts have already been made to deal honestly

and fairly with this tragic situation, and to ensure that children — whom our Lord loves so deeply (cf. *Mk* 10:14), and who are our greatest treasure — can grow up in a safe environment. These efforts to protect children must continue. Yesterday I spoke with your Bishops about this. Today I encourage each of you to do what you can to foster healing and reconciliation, and to assist those who have been hurt. Also, I ask you to love your priests, and to affirm them in the excellent work that they do. And above all, pray that the Holy Spirit will pour out his gifts upon the Church, the gifts that lead to conversion, forgiveness and growth in holiness.

Pope Benedict XVI's homily
at St. Patrick's Cathedral

Two days after the Mass in Washington, D.C., and a day after his address to the United Nations on the recognition of the unity of the human family and need for attention to the innate dignity of every man and woman, the Holy Father celebrated a Votive Mass at St. Patrick's Cathedral for the Universal Church with priests and men and women religious.

In a profound reflection on the Church, the pontiff used the immense and beloved Gothic masterpiece of St. Patrick's Cathedral as a model for the great spiritual legacy to which the Church in the United States was the heir. As he explained, the cathedral's chief builder, Archbishop John Hughes, intended it to inspire the young Church in America "to bring the best of that heritage to the building up of Christ's body in this land." The pope then used the image of the building itself to describe the Church.

He began by pointing out the stained glass in the church, adopting an idea that other writers have developed, including Nathaniel Hawthorne. From the exterior, the windows seem dark and even dreary. Upon entering the church, however, the windows come alive so that one realizes that it is "only from the inside, from the experience of faith and ecclesial life, that we see the Church as she truly is: flooded with grace, resplendent in beauty, adorned by the manifold gifts of the Spirit."

The task of leading others into the Church is not an easy one in the modern world. Like the stained glass windows, "from the outside" the faith can seem a mystery and even uninviting. For those within the Church, the light that floods through the windows can be dimmed "by the sins and weaknesses of her members" and also "by the obstacles encountered in a society which sometimes seems to have forgotten God and to resent even the most elementary demands of Christian morality."

A second aspect of the St. Patrick's architecture is that, like all Gothic cathedrals, the very construction involved is accomplished through the bringing together into unity "exact and harmonious proportions." This makes the cathedral a symbol of "the unity of God's creation." He then asks the question, "Does this not bring to mind our need to see all things with the eyes of faith, and thus to grasp them in their truest perspective, in the unity of God's eternal plan?"

The challenges to unity, of course, are everywhere to be seen, and Benedict cited the disappointment and experience of division that took place in the Church after the Second Vatican Council among generations, different groups and different members of the same faith. The unity of vision and purpose, however, was a secret to the growth and success of the Church in the United States.

In his homily at the Mass in Washington, the pope used hope as his introduction to addressing the sex abuse scandal. In his homily at St. Patrick's, he used unity as his context. This was a logical application of the theme — for, as Vicar of Christ, he was deeply concerned about the dangers to unity that the crisis has posed for the Church, from both the divisions created between priests and laypeople (through fear and mistrust) and those between priests and their bishops.

Extending the image of unity further, the pope applied one final observation about the architecture of St. Patrick's. The unity of a Gothic cathedral, he describes, is not some static unity as is seen with a classical temple; it is "a unity born of the dynamic tension of diverse forces which impel the architecture upward, pointing it to heaven." This, also, is a symbol for the Church's unity that is "a living body composed of many different members, each with its own role and purpose." The members of that living body must reverence the gifts of each other that need, nevertheless, "to be rightly ordered in the service of the Church's mission."

Votive Mass for the Universal Church
Homily of His Holiness Benedict XVI
St. Patrick's Cathedral, New York
Saturday, April 19, 2008

Dear Brothers and Sisters in Christ,

With great affection in the Lord, I greet all of you, who represent the Bishops, priests and deacons, the men and women in consecrated life, and the seminarians of the United States. I thank Cardinal Egan for his warm welcome and the good wishes which he has expressed in your name as I begin the fourth year of my papal ministry. I am happy to celebrate this Mass with you, who have been chosen by the Lord, who have answered his call, and who devote your lives to the pursuit of holiness, the spread of the Gospel and the building up of the Church in faith, hope and love.

Gathered as we are in this historic cathedral, how can we not think of the countless men and women who have gone before us, who labored for the growth of the Church in the United States, and left us a lasting legacy of faith and good works? In today's first reading we saw how, in the power of the Holy Spirit, the Apostles went forth from the Upper Room to proclaim God's mighty works to people of every nation and tongue. In this country, the Church's mission has always involved drawing people "from every nation under heaven" (cf. *Acts* 2:5) into spiritual unity, and enriching the Body of Christ by the variety of their gifts. As we give thanks for these precious past blessings, and look to the challenges of the future, let us implore from God the grace of a new Pentecost for the Church in America. May tongues of fire, combining burning love of God and neighbor with zeal for the spread of Christ's Kingdom, descend on all present!

[. . .]

For all of us, I think, one of the great disappointments which followed the Second Vatican Council, with its call for a greater engagement in the Church's mission to the world, has been the experience of division between different groups, different generations, different members of the same religious family. We can only move forward if we turn our gaze together to Christ! In the light of faith, we will then discover the wisdom and strength needed to open ourselves to points of view which may not necessarily conform to our own ideas or assumptions. Thus we can value the perspectives of others, be they younger or older than ourselves, and ultimately hear "what the Spirit is saying" to us and to the Church (cf. *Rev* 2:7). In this way, we will move together towards that true spiritual renewal desired by the Council, a renewal which can only strengthen the Church in that holiness and unity indispensable for the effective proclamation of the Gospel in today's world.

Was not this unity of vision and purpose — rooted in faith and a spirit of constant conversion and self-sacrifice — the secret of the impressive growth of the Church in this country? We need but think of the remarkable accomplishment of that exemplary American priest, the Venerable Michael McGivney, whose vision and zeal led to the establishment of the Knights of Columbus, or of the legacy of the generations of religious and priests who quietly devoted their lives to serving the People of God in countless schools, hospitals, and parishes.

Here, within the context of our need for the perspective given by faith, and for unity and cooperation in the work of building up the Church, I would like say a word about the sexual abuse that has caused so much suffering. I have already had occasion to speak of this, and of the resulting damage to the community of the faithful. Here I simply wish to assure you, dear priests and religious, of my spiritual closeness as you strive to respond with Christian hope to the continuing challenges that this situation presents. I join you in praying that this will be a time of purification for each and every particular Church and religious community, and a time for healing. And I also encourage you to cooperate with your Bishops who continue to work effectively to resolve this issue. May our Lord Jesus Christ grant the Church in America a renewed sense of unity and purpose, as all — Bishops, clergy, religious, and laity — move forward in hope, in love for the truth and for one another.

Pope Benedict XVI's homily at the Mass at the Cathedral of Sydney

A week after his in-flight press conference and many of the events of World Youth Day, the Holy Father celebrated Mass at St. Mary's Cathedral in Sydney with the bishops of Australia. Pope Benedict took the opportunity to speak of the scandal.

The Mass was to celebrate the dedication of the new altar of St. Mary's Cathedral, and the pontiff used the event as the theme for his homily. He taught that "every altar is a symbol of Jesus Christ, present in the midst of his Church as priest, altar and victim (cf. *Preface of Easter* V)." According to the Holy Father, the Church teaches us that we have also been set apart, like the altar, "for the service of God and the building up of his Kingdom." Sadly, today the world sets God aside, and his name "is passed over in silence, religion is reduced to private devotion, and faith is shunned in the public square."

And yet, "the question of God will never be silenced" because faith instructs us that we are God's creatures and that ultimately the final measure against which humanity must be measured is the Cross. The truth that we find ourselves only by giving our lives away is a mystery of faith, but it demands what the Holy Father called "continual conversion, a sacrificial death to self which is the condition for belonging fully to God, a change of mind and heart which brings true freedom and a new breadth of vision."

Within the context of renewal, the pope proceeded to discuss the sex abuse scandal that has caused great sadness and upheaval in the Australian Catholic community. As he had in other addresses, the pontiff used the carefully chosen word "shame."

He concluded by speaking directly to the seminarians and young religious. He reminded them that they had "set out on a particular path of consecration, grounded in your Baptism and undertaken in response to the Lord's personal call. You have committed yourselves, in different ways, to accepting Christ's invitation to follow him, to leave all behind, and to devote your lives to the pursuit of holiness and the service of his people." He returned to the theme of the altar and called on them to become "living altars, where Christ's sacrificial love is made present as an inspiration and a source of spiritual nourishment to everyone you meet."

Eucharistic Celebration with Bishops, Seminarians, and Novices
Homily of His Holiness Benedict XVI
St. Mary's Cathedral, Sydney, Saturday, July 19, 2008

[excerpt]

Dear Brothers and Sisters,

In this noble cathedral I rejoice to greet my brother Bishops and priests, and the deacons, religious, and laity of the archdiocese of Sydney. In a very special way, my greeting goes to the seminarians and young religious who are present among us. Like the young Israelites in today's first reading, they are a sign of hope and renewal for God's people; and, like those young Israelites, they will have the task of building up the Lord's house in the coming generation. As we admire this magnificent edifice, how can we not think of all those ranks of priests, religious and faithful laity who, each in his or her own way, contributed to the building up of the Church in Australia? Our thoughts turn in particular to those settler families to whom Father Jeremiah O'Flynn entrusted the Blessed Sacrament at his departure, a "small flock" which cherished and preserved that precious treasure, passing it on to the succeeding generations who raised this great tabernacle to the glory of God. Let us rejoice in their fidelity and perseverance, and dedicate ourselves to carrying on their labors for the spread of the Gospel, the conversion of hearts and the growth of the Church in holiness, unity, and charity!

[. . .]

Dear friends, may this celebration, in the presence of the Successor of Peter, be a moment of rededication and renewal for the whole Church in Australia! Here I would like to pause to acknowledge the shame which we have all felt as a result of the sexual abuse of minors by some clergy and religious in this country. Indeed, I am deeply sorry for the pain and suffering the victims have endured, and I assure them that, as their Pastor, I too share in their suffering. These misdeeds, which constitute so grave a betrayal of trust, deserve unequivocal condemnation. They have caused great pain and have damaged the Church's witness. I ask all of you to support and assist your Bishops, and to work together with them in combating this evil. Victims should receive compassion and care, and those responsible for these evils must be brought to justice. It is an urgent priority to promote a safer and more wholesome environment, especially for young people. In these days marked by the celebration of World Youth Day, we are reminded of how precious a treasure has been entrusted to us in our young people, and how great a part of the Church's mission in this country has been dedicated to their education and care. As the Church in Australia continues, in the spirit of the Gospel, to address effectively this serious pastoral challenge, I join you in praying that this time of purification will bring about healing, reconciliation and ever greater fidelity to the moral demands of the Gospel.

I wish now to turn to the seminarians and young religious in our midst, with a special word of affection and encouragement. Dear friends: with great generosity you have set out on a particular path of consecration, grounded in your Baptism and undertaken in response to the Lord's personal call. You have committed yourselves, in different ways, to accepting Christ's invitation to follow him, to leave all behind, and to devote your lives to the pursuit of holiness and the service of his people.

Pope Benedict XVI's
Pastoral Letter to the Catholics of Ireland

The crisis confronting the Catholic Church in Ireland had been a concern for Pope Benedict for years, and his efforts to confront and help resolve the situation culminated with a "Pastoral Letter to the Catholics of Ireland" that was issued on March 19, 2010, with the request that it be read with attention and in its entirety.

The Holy Father expressed his alarm at the gravity of the situation in the very first paragraph of the letter, when he wrote:

> I have been deeply disturbed by the information which has come to light regarding the abuse of children and vulnerable young people by members of the Church in Ireland, particularly by priests and religious. I can only share in the dismay and the sense of betrayal that so many of you have experienced on learning of these sinful and criminal acts and the way Church authorities in Ireland dealt with them.

He then placed his own response to the crisis within the wider pattern of events of the last few years. He pointed to the meeting in Rome with the Irish bishops, where he demanded

> . . . [that they] give an account of their handling of these matters in the past and to outline the steps they have taken to respond to this grave situation. Together with senior officials of the Roman Curia, I listened to what they had to say, both individually and as a group, as they offered

an analysis of mistakes made and lessons learned, and a description of the programmes and protocols now in place.

He once again wrote bluntly about the situation, citing as his reasons for writing the Letter: both "the gravity of these offences, and the often inadequate response to them on the part of the ecclesiastical authorities in your country," and as a way to express his "closeness to you and to propose a path of healing, renewal, and reparation." This candor made the Letter an immediately striking papal document, and this frankness was matched by the sincere tone of grief and sorrow and the pope's desire to provide healing and reconciliation to a stricken part of his flock.

After reminding the Irish of the immense legacy of faith in the Islands, and the immense contributions made by Irish missionaries to European civilization and beyond, the pope detailed the many challenges to that faith in Ireland — largely the result of unprecedented social change and the decline of some areas of Church life, including adherence to traditional devotional and sacramental practices. Pope Benedict diagnosed the problem by centering these declines in poor moral and spiritual formation in seminaries and novitiates, a social tendency to place excessive deference to the clergy and other authority figures, and a mistaken belief in the need to protect the reputation of the Church that led to failures in dealing with the problems of sexual abuse among some in the clergy by applying the canonical penalties that were in place.

The subsequent structure of the Letter was built around the specific elements of the Catholic community in Ireland that have been most severely impacted by the crisis: the victims of abuse and their families; the priests and religious who have abused children; parents; the children and young people of Ireland; the priests and religious of Ireland; the bishops; and all the faithful of Ireland.

The pontiff finished the letter with a series of concrete steps for the spiritual renewal and healing of the Church in Ireland. These included: devoting Friday penances for a period of one year to healing, rediscovering the sacrament of Reconciliation, and participating in Eucharistic adoration. He also announced his plan for an apostolic visitation of certain dioceses, as well as seminaries and religious congregations, and a nationwide Mission to be held for all bishops, priests, and religious.

The unprecedented papal letter to the Catholics of Ireland marked a decisive moment not only in the long and terrible history of the crisis in Ireland but in the Church's response to clergy sexual abuse. It is unfortunate that this heartfelt, clear and unambiguous letter — the first of its kind in Church history — has been so overlooked in the furor surrounding the pope.

Pastoral Letter of the Holy Father, Pope Benedict XVI to the Catholics of Ireland

1. Dear Brothers and Sisters of the Church in Ireland, it is with great concern that I write to you as Pastor of the universal Church. Like yourselves, I have been deeply disturbed by the information which has come to light regarding the abuse of children and vulnerable young people by members of the Church in Ireland, particularly by priests and religious. I can only share in the dismay and the sense of betrayal that so many of you have experienced on learning of these sinful and criminal acts and the way Church authorities in Ireland dealt with them.

As you know, I recently invited the Irish bishops to a meeting here in Rome to give an account of their handling of these matters in the past and to outline the steps they have taken to respond to this grave situation. Together with senior officials of the Roman Curia, I listened to what they had to say, both individually and as a group, as they offered an analysis of mistakes made and lessons learned, and a description of the programs and protocols now in place. Our discussions were frank and constructive. I am confident that, as a result, the bishops will now be in a stronger position to carry forward the work of repairing past injustices and confronting the broader issues associated with the abuse of minors in a way consonant with the demands of justice and the teachings of the Gospel.

2. For my part, considering the gravity of these offences, and the often inadequate response to them on the part of the ecclesiastical authorities in your country, I have decided to write this Pastoral Letter to express my closeness to you and to propose a path of healing, renewal and reparation.

It is true, as many in your country have pointed out, that the problem of child abuse is peculiar neither to Ireland nor to the Church. Nevertheless, the task you now face is to address the problem of abuse that has occurred within the Irish Catholic community, and to do so with courage and determination. No one imagines that this painful situation will be resolved swiftly. Real progress has been made, yet much more remains to be done. Perseverance and prayer are needed, with great trust in the healing power of God's grace.

At the same time, I must also express my conviction that, in order to recover from this grievous wound, the Church in Ireland must first acknowledge before the Lord and before others the serious sins committed against defenseless children. Such an acknowledgement, accompanied by sincere sorrow for the damage caused to these victims and their families must lead to a concerted effort to ensure the protection of children from similar crimes in the future.

As you take up the challenges of this hour, I ask you to remember "the rock from which you were hewn" (*Is* 51:1). Reflect upon the generous, often heroic, contributions made by past generations of Irish men and women to the Church and to humanity as a whole, and let this provide the impetus for honest self-examination and a committed program of ecclesial and individual renewal. It is my prayer that, assisted by the intercession of her many saints and purified through penance, the Church in Ireland will overcome the present crisis and become once more a convincing witness to the truth and the goodness of Almighty God, made manifest in his Son Jesus Christ.

3. Historically, the Catholics of Ireland have proved an enormous force for good at home and abroad. Celtic monks like Saint Columbanus spread the Gospel in Western Europe and laid the foundations of medieval monastic culture. The ideals of holiness, charity and transcendent wisdom born of the Christian faith found expression in the building of churches and monasteries and the establishment of schools, libraries and hospitals, all of which helped to consolidate the spiritual identity of Europe. Those Irish missionaries drew their strength and inspiration from the firm faith, strong leadership and upright morals of the Church in their native land.

From the sixteenth century on, Catholics in Ireland endured a long period of persecution, during which they struggled to keep the flame of faith alive in dangerous and difficult circumstances. Saint Oliver Plunkett, the martyred Archbishop of Armagh, is the most famous example of a host of courageous sons and daughters of Ireland who were willing to lay down their lives out of fidelity to the Gospel. After Catholic Emancipation, the Church was free to grow once more. Families and countless individuals who had preserved the faith in times of trial became the catalyst for the great resurgence of Irish Catholicism in the nineteenth century. The Church provided education, especially for the poor, and this was to make a major contribution to Irish society. Among the fruits of the new Catholic schools was a rise in vocations: generations of missionary priests, sisters and brothers left their homeland to serve in every continent, especially in the English-speaking world. They were remarkable not only for their great numbers, but for the strength of their faith and the steadfastness of their pastoral commitment. Many dioceses, especially in Africa, America and Australia, benefited from the presence of Irish clergy and religious who preached the Gospel and established parishes, schools and universities, clinics and hospitals that served both Catholics and the community at large, with particular attention to the needs of the poor.

In almost every family in Ireland, there has been someone — a son or a daughter, an aunt or an uncle — who has given his or her life to the Church. Irish families rightly esteem and cherish their loved ones who have dedicated their lives to Christ, sharing the gift of faith with others, and putting that faith into action in loving service of God and neighbor.

4. In recent decades, however, the Church in your country has had to confront new and serious challenges to the faith arising from the rapid transformation and secularization of Irish society. Fast-paced social change has occurred, often adversely affecting people's traditional adherence to Catholic teaching and values. All too often, the sacramental and devotional practices that sustain faith and enable it to grow, such as frequent confession, daily prayer and annual retreats, were neglected. Significant too was the tendency during this period, also on the part of priests and religious, to adopt ways of thinking and assessing secular realities without sufficient reference to the Gospel. The program of renewal proposed by the Second Vatican Council was sometimes misinterpreted and indeed, in the light of the profound social changes that were taking place, it was far from easy to know how best to implement it. In particular, there was a well-intentioned but misguided tendency to avoid penal approaches to canonically irregular situations. It is in this overall context that we must try to understand the disturbing problem of child sexual abuse, which has contributed in no small measure to the weakening of faith and the loss of respect for the Church and her teachings.

Only by examining carefully the many elements that gave rise to the present crisis can a clear-sighted diagnosis of its causes be undertaken and effective remedies be found. Certainly, among the contributing factors we can include: inadequate procedures for determining the suitability of candidates for the priesthood and the religious life; insufficient human, moral, intellectual and spiritual formation in seminaries and novitiates; a tendency in society to favour the clergy and other authority figures; and a misplaced concern for the reputation of the Church and the avoidance of scandal, resulting in failure to apply existing canonical penalties and to safeguard the dignity of every person. Urgent action is needed to address these factors, which have had such tragic consequences in the lives of victims and their families, and have obscured the light of the Gospel to a degree that not even centuries of persecution succeeded in doing.

5. On several occasions since my election to the See of Peter, I have met with victims of sexual abuse, as indeed I am ready to do in the future. I have sat with them, I have listened to their stories, I have acknowledged their suffering, and I have prayed with them and for them. Earlier in my pontificate, in my concern to address this matter, I asked the bishops of Ireland, "to establish the truth of what happened in the past, to take whatever steps are necessary to prevent it from occurring again, to ensure that the principles of justice are fully respected, and above all, to bring healing to the victims and to all those affected by these egregious crimes" (*Address to the Bishops of Ireland*, 28 October 2006).

With this Letter, I wish to exhort *all of you*, as God's people in Ireland, to reflect on the wounds inflicted on Christ's body, the sometimes painful remedies needed to bind and heal them, and the need for unity, charity and mutual support in the long-term process of restoration and ecclesial renewal. I now turn to you with words that come from my heart, and I wish to speak to each of you individually and to all of you as brothers and sisters in the Lord.

6. To the victims of abuse and their families

You have suffered grievously and I am truly sorry. I know that nothing can undo the wrong you have endured. Your trust has been betrayed and your dignity has been violated. Many of you found that, when you were courageous enough to speak of what happened to you, no one would listen. Those of you who were abused in residential institutions must have felt that there was no escape from your sufferings. It is understandable that you find it hard to forgive or be reconciled with the Church. In her name, I openly express the shame and remorse that we all feel. At the same time, I ask you not to lose hope. It is in the communion of the Church that we encounter the person of Jesus Christ, who was himself a victim of injustice and sin. Like you, he still bears the wounds of his own unjust suffering. He understands the depths of your pain and its enduring effect upon your lives and your relationships, including your relationship with the Church. I know some of you find it difficult even to enter the doors of a church after all that has occurred. Yet Christ's own wounds, transformed by his redemptive sufferings, are the very means by which the power of evil is broken and we are reborn to life and hope. I believe deeply in the healing power of his self-sacrificing love — even in the darkest and most hopeless situations — to bring liberation and the promise of a new beginning.

Speaking to you as a pastor concerned for the good of all God's children, I humbly ask you to consider what I have said. I pray that, by drawing nearer to Christ and by participating in the life of his Church — a Church purified by penance and renewed in pastoral charity — you will come to rediscover Christ's infinite love for each one of you. I am confident that in this way you will be able to find reconciliation, deep inner healing and peace.

7. To priests and religious who have abused children

You betrayed the trust that was placed in you by innocent young people and their parents, and you must answer for it before Almighty God and before properly constituted tribunals. You have forfeited the esteem of the people of Ireland and brought shame and dishonor upon your confreres. Those of you who are priests violated the sanctity of the sacrament of Holy Orders in which Christ makes himself present in us and in our actions. Together with the immense harm done to victims, great damage has been done to the Church and to the public perception of the priesthood and religious life.

I urge you to examine your conscience, take responsibility for the sins you have committed, and humbly express your sorrow. Sincere repentance opens the door to God's forgiveness and the grace of true amendment. By offering prayers and penances for those you have wronged, you should seek to atone personally for your actions. Christ's redeeming sacrifice has the power to forgive even the gravest of sins, and to bring forth good from even the most terrible evil. At the same time, God's justice summons us to give an account of our actions and to conceal nothing. Openly acknowledge your guilt, submit yourselves to the demands of justice, but do not despair of God's mercy.

8. To parents

You have been deeply shocked to learn of the terrible things that took place in what ought to be the safest and most secure environment of all. In today's world it is not easy to build a home and to bring up children. They deserve to grow up in security, loved and cherished, with a strong sense of their identity and worth. They have a right to be educated in authentic moral values rooted in the dignity of the human person, to be inspired by the truth of our Catholic faith and to learn ways of behaving and acting that lead to healthy self-esteem and lasting happiness. This noble but demanding task is entrusted in the first place to you, their parents. I urge you to play your part in ensuring the best possible care of children, both at home and in society as a whole, while the Church, for her part, continues to implement the measures adopted in recent years to protect young people in parish and school environments. As you carry out your vital responsibilities, be assured that I remain close to you and I offer you the support of my prayers.

9. To the children and young people of Ireland

I wish to offer you a particular word of encouragement. Your experience of the Church is very different from that of your parents and grandparents. The world has changed greatly since they were your age. Yet all people, in every generation, are called to travel the same path through life, whatever their circumstances may be. We are all scandalized by the sins and failures of some of the Church's members, particularly those who were chosen especially to guide and serve young people. But it is *in the Church* that you will find Jesus Christ, who is the same yesterday, today and forever (cf. *Heb* 13:8). He loves you and he has offered himself on the cross for you. Seek a personal relationship with him within the communion of his Church, for he will never betray your trust! He alone can satisfy your deepest longings and give your lives their fullest meaning by directing them to the service of others. Keep your eyes fixed on Jesus and his goodness, and shelter the flame of faith in your heart. Together with your fellow Catholics in Ireland, I look to you to be faithful disciples of our Lord and to bring your much-needed enthusiasm and idealism to the rebuilding and renewal of our beloved Church.

10. To the priests and religious of Ireland

All of us are suffering as a result of the sins of our confreres who betrayed a sacred trust or failed to deal justly and responsibly with allegations of abuse. In view of the outrage and indignation which this has provoked, not only among the lay faithful but among yourselves and your religious communities, many of you feel personally discouraged, even abandoned. I am also aware that in some people's eyes you are tainted by association, and viewed as if you were somehow responsible for the misdeeds of others. At this painful time, I want to acknowledge the dedication of your priestly and religious lives and apostolates, and I invite you to reaffirm your faith in Christ, your love of his Church and your confidence in the Gospel's promise of redemption, forgiveness and interior renewal. In this way, you will demonstrate for all to see that where sin abounds, grace abounds all the more (cf. *Rom* 5:20).

I know that many of you are disappointed, bewildered, and angered by the way these matters have been handled by some of your superiors. Yet, it is essential that you cooperate closely with those in authority and help to ensure that the measures adopted to respond to the crisis will be truly evangelical, just and effective. Above all, I urge you to become ever more clearly men and women of prayer, courageously following the path of conversion, purification and reconciliation. In this way, the Church in Ireland will draw new life and vitality from your witness to the Lord's redeeming power made visible in your lives.

11. To my brother bishops

It cannot be denied that some of you and your predecessors failed, at times grievously, to apply the long-established norms of canon law to the crime of child abuse. Serious mistakes were made in responding to allegations. I recognize how difficult it was to grasp the extent and complexity of the problem, to obtain reliable information and to make the right decisions in the light of conflicting expert advice. Nevertheless, it must be admitted that grave errors of judgment were made and failures of leadership occurred. All this has seriously undermined your credibility and effectiveness. I appreciate the efforts you have made to remedy past mistakes and to guarantee that they do not happen again. Besides fully implementing the norms of canon law in addressing cases of child abuse, continue to cooperate with the civil authorities in their area of competence. Clearly, religious superiors should do likewise. They too have taken part in recent discussions here in Rome with a view to establishing a clear and consistent approach to these matters. It is imperative that the child safety norms of the Church in Ireland be continually revised and updated and that they be applied fully and impartially in conformity with canon law.

Only decisive action carried out with complete honesty and transparency will restore the respect and good will of the Irish people towards the Church to which we have consecrated our lives. This must arise, first and foremost, from your own self-examination, inner purification and spiritual renewal. The Irish people rightly expect you to be men of God, to be holy, to live simply, to pursue personal conversion daily. For them, in the words of Saint Augustine, you are a bishop; yet with them you are called to be a follower of Christ (cf. *Sermon* 340, 1). I therefore exhort you to renew your sense of accountability before God, to grow in solidarity with your people and to deepen your pastoral concern for all the members of your flock. In particular, I ask you to be attentive to the spiritual and moral lives of each one of your priests. Set them an example by your own lives, be close to them, listen to their concerns, offer them encouragement at this difficult time and stir up the flame of their love for Christ and their commitment to the service of their brothers and sisters.

The lay faithful, too, should be encouraged to play their proper part in the life of the Church. See that they are formed in such a way that they can offer an articulate and convincing account of the Gospel in the midst of modern society (cf. *1 Pet*

3:15) and cooperate more fully in the Church's life and mission. This in turn will help you once again become credible leaders and witnesses to the redeeming truth of Christ.

12. To all the faithful of Ireland

A young person's experience of the Church should always bear fruit in a personal and life-giving encounter with Jesus Christ within a loving, nourishing community. In this environment, young people should be encouraged to grow to their full human and spiritual stature, to aspire to high ideals of holiness, charity and truth, and to draw inspiration from the riches of a great religious and cultural tradition. In our increasingly secularized society, where even we Christians often find it difficult to speak of the transcendent dimension of our existence, we need to find new ways to pass on to young people the beauty and richness of friendship with Jesus Christ in the communion of his Church. In confronting the present crisis, measures to deal justly with individual crimes are essential, yet on their own they are not enough: a new vision is needed, to inspire present and future generations to treasure the gift of our common faith. By treading the path marked out by the Gospel, by observing the commandments and by conforming your lives ever more closely to the figure of Jesus Christ, you will surely experience the profound renewal that is so urgently needed at this time. I invite you all to persevere along this path.

13. Dear brothers and sisters in Christ, it is out of deep concern for all of you at this painful time in which the fragility of the human condition has been so starkly revealed that I have wished to offer these words of encouragement and support. I hope that you will receive them as a sign of my spiritual closeness and my confidence in your ability to respond to the challenges of the present hour by drawing renewed inspiration and strength from Ireland's noble traditions of fidelity to the Gospel, perseverance in the faith and steadfastness in the pursuit

of holiness. In solidarity with all of you, I am praying earnestly that, by God's grace, the wounds afflicting so many individuals and families may be healed and that the Church in Ireland may experience a season of rebirth and spiritual renewal.

14. I now wish to propose to you some concrete initiatives to address the situation.

At the conclusion of my meeting with the Irish bishops, I asked that Lent this year be set aside as a time to pray for an outpouring of God's mercy and the Holy Spirit's gifts of holiness and strength upon the Church in your country. I now invite all of you to devote your Friday penances, for a period of one year, between now and Easter 2011, to this intention. I ask you to offer up your fasting, your prayer, your reading of Scripture and your works of mercy in order to obtain the grace of healing and renewal for the Church in Ireland. I encourage you to discover anew the sacrament of Reconciliation and to avail yourselves more frequently of the transforming power of its grace.

Particular attention should also be given to Eucharistic adoration, and in every diocese there should be churches or chapels specifically devoted to this purpose. I ask parishes, seminaries, religious houses and monasteries to organize periods of Eucharistic adoration, so that all have an opportunity to take part. Through intense prayer before the real presence of the Lord, you can make reparation for the sins of abuse that have done so much harm, at the same time imploring the grace of renewed strength and a deeper sense of mission on the part of all bishops, priests, religious and lay faithful.

I am confident that this program will lead to a rebirth of the Church in Ireland in the fullness of God's own truth, for it is the truth that sets us free (cf. *Jn* 8:32).

Furthermore, having consulted and prayed about the matter, I intend to hold an Apostolic Visitation of certain dioceses in Ireland, as well as seminaries and religious congregations.

Arrangements for the Visitation, which is intended to assist the local Church on her path of renewal, will be made in cooperation with the competent offices of the Roman Curia and the Irish Episcopal Conference. The details will be announced in due course.

I also propose that a nationwide Mission be held for all bishops, priests and religious. It is my hope that, by drawing on the expertise of experienced preachers and retreat-givers from Ireland and from elsewhere, and by exploring anew the conciliar documents, the liturgical rites of ordination and profession, and recent pontifical teaching, you will come to a more profound appreciation of your respective vocations, so as to rediscover the roots of your faith in Jesus Christ and to drink deeply from the springs of living water that he offers you through his Church.

In this Year for Priests, I commend to you most particularly the figure of Saint John Mary Vianney, who had such a rich understanding of the mystery of the priesthood. "The priest," he wrote, "holds the key to the treasures of heaven: it is he who opens the door: he is the steward of the good Lord; the administrator of his goods." The Curé d'Ars understood well how greatly blessed a community is when served by a good and holy priest: "A good shepherd, a pastor after God's heart, is the greatest treasure which the good Lord can grant to a parish, and one of the most precious gifts of divine mercy." Through the intercession of Saint John Mary Vianney, may the priesthood in Ireland be revitalized, and may the whole Church in Ireland grow in appreciation for the great gift of the priestly ministry.

I take this opportunity to thank in anticipation all those who will be involved in the work of organizing the Apostolic Visitation and the Mission, as well as the many men and women throughout Ireland already working for the safety of children in church environments. Since the time when the gravity and extent of the problem of child sexual abuse in Catholic institutions first began to be fully grasped, the Church has done an immense amount of work in many parts of the world in order to address and remedy it. While no effort should be spared in improving and updating existing procedures, I am encouraged by the fact that the current safeguarding practices adopted by local Churches are being seen, in some parts of the world, as a model for other institutions to follow.

I wish to conclude this Letter with a special *Prayer for the Church in Ireland*, which I send to you with the care of a father for his children and with the affection of a fellow Christian, scandalized and hurt by what has occurred in our beloved Church. As you make use of this prayer in your families, parishes and communities, may the Blessed Virgin Mary protect and guide each of you to a closer union with her Son, crucified and risen. With great affection and unswerving confidence in God's promises, I cordially impart to all of you my Apostolic Blessing as a pledge of strength and peace in the Lord.

From the Vatican, 19 March 2010, on the Solemnity of Saint Joseph

Benedictus PP. XVI

Prayer for the Church in Ireland

God of our fathers,
>   renew us in the faith which is our life and salvation,
>   the hope which promises forgiveness and interior renewal,
>   the charity which purifies and opens our hearts
>   to love you, and in you, each of our brothers and sisters.

Lord Jesus Christ,
>   may the Church in Ireland renew her age-old commitment
>   to the education of our young people in the way of truth
>   and goodness, holiness and generous service to society.

Holy Spirit, comforter, advocate and guide,
>   inspire a new springtime of holiness and apostolic zeal
>   for the Church in Ireland.

May our sorrow and our tears,
>   our sincere effort to redress past wrongs,
>   and our firm purpose of amendment
>   bear an abundant harvest of grace
>   for the deepening of the faith
>   in our families, parishes, schools and communities,
>   for the spiritual progress of Irish society,
>   and the growth of charity, justice, joy and peace
>   within the whole human family.

To you, Triune God,
>   confident in the loving protection of Mary,
>   Queen of Ireland, our Mother,
>   and of Saint Patrick, Saint Brigid and all the saints,
>   do we entrust ourselves, our children,
>   and the needs of the Church in Ireland.

Amen.